. . . . and to my family . . . Daddy did it!!

Restoring the Music
Published by
Watersprings Media House, LLC
P.O. Box 1284
Olive Branch, MS 38654
www.waterspringsmedia.com

Contact publisher for bulk orders and permission requests.

Copyrights © 2018 by Delroy A. Brooks. All rights reserved.

No part of this publication may be reproduced, distributed, or transmitted in any form or by any means, including photo-copying, recording, or other electronic or mechanical meth-ods, without the prior written permission of the publisher, except in the case of brief quotations embodied in critical reviews and certain other noncommercial uses permitted by copyright law.

Scripture quotations are taken from the Holy Bible, New International Version®. NIV® Copyright 1973, 1978, 1984 by International Bible Society. Used by permission of Zondervan. All rights reserved.

Printed in the United States of America.

Library of Congress Control Number: 2018961062

ISBN-13: 978-1-948877-07-7

Restoring the Music

Developing Young Adult Leaders for the Local Church

by

Delroy A. Brooks

Watersprings
PUBLISHING

Table of Contents

Introduction 6

Chapter 1: A Little Music History 10

Chapter 2: What Has Leadership Sounded Like?.............. 13

Chapter 3: The Music of Youth and Young Adult Ministry.... 27

Chapter 4: Can You Hear Me Now? 36

Chapter 5: Finding the Music Together 60

Chapter 6: Outro 81

Author Bio 86

Connect with Author 86

INTRODUCTION

I grew up in a Black church. Although we were Seventh Day Adventists, we were still emotive and emotional in our worship. We had all the trappings of mainline African American churches that worship on Sunday's: a children's choir, youth choir, young adult choir, and the adult choir. Each choir represented a different segment of the church population. As I grew, I believed that what I saw exemplified in our choirs would also be expressed in the leadership of the church. You get older, you move from this choir to that choir. Youth were not barred from singing in the older choirs, as a matter of fact, we had to sing with the older choirs every Christmas, Easter, and any 'special days' on the church calendar. And although we could sing with the older group, it would be many years before a young adult would be allowed to lead the mass choir.

There was a piece missing then and a piece missing now as it relates to youth and young adults leading in our African American (Black) churches. There is an expectation to accomplish, yet no mechanism to foster that accomplishment. My own travel away from home and subsequent return to my church informs much of what I do in ministry. It is the impetus of my desire to find what we may have been missing at my home church and many of the churches that I have been a part of now that I am located in sunny Southern California. We don't have as many choirs anymore. We still have the children, our youth have chosen work in the background, and our young adults are missing altogether.

Along with my passion for youth ministry, music has always been a major part of my life. From learning piano, practicing guitar, and singing in some of those choirs that I referenced earlier, music has been pretty significant in my development as a person, pastor, and today, father. My experiences as a young adult leader are all filtered through musical experiences in my formative years. At thirteen, I joined a choir that had never existed in my church. A teenager saw that there were other teens who had some talent and were not old enough to be in the gospel choir and were too old for the children's choir. There was a lot of resistance in those days to a bunch of teens hanging out at the church, even though all we wanted to do was be in community, be accepted by our church family, and be supported in our activities. When I went to college, I was a part of another historical change: a student led choir on the campus of the College. Prior to the forming of this group, all other choirs were under the auspices of student government, or the school bureaucracy. This new choir, which still exists today, just wanted to be in community, be accepted by our school officially, and be supported in our activities. Throughout this book I will use musical terms, because music like leadership, is an art. It is my intention to present a way the music of young adult leadership can play in our urban churches.

Youth ministry in my tradition began with teenagers, Luther Warren and Harry Fenner, ages 14 and 17 respectively, who in 1879 were "concerned about the spiritual needs of their peers both inside and outside the church." Their desire for their peers led them to create the youth ministry arm of the church. They were credited for beginning the music of youth ministry within the SDA tradition. What began with zeal seems to have lost its zest. Today we see young people leaving in droves. There are those like me, who still remain. They've stuck around, got involved and became leaders. Was there something in our DNA that made us different? Is there anything to learn from those who stayed? My guess has always been there was a level of treatment of specific individuals, whether explicit or implicit, that let them feel like there was something that they could do. This method however, has never been to my knowledge, written down for replication or broadened for systematic duplication.

Today there is a disconnection between the youth and the leadership of the church. With fewer and fewer young people attending church, a hole has been created in the membership where the young people used to be. With that we are also seeing a growing generation gap in churches that impacts leadership and how youth are and are not transitioning into leadership at the local level. What used to be a natural occurrence changed somewhere. As a result, there are some problems that arise.

Naturally, older members may have diminished physical capacity to engage in some of the tasks of church ministry. But that is not all that is lost in the aging of the congregation. We also lose a critical leadership transfer, or trade from one generation to the next, when our youth check out after high school and the young adults are not involved. We must admit that there is a problem. The question for me then becomes is there something that can be done in the church, the African American church in particular, to stave off this graying of the church? What are some ways we can transition our existing youth and young adults into leadership that could infuse life and energy into all aspects of the local church?

This exodus from the church among young people is not exclusive to African Americans in my tradition. It affects many ethnicities and can erode the health of the church over time.

Further affecting the health and stability of the church in years to come is the low likelihood of teen's remaining churched. Barely one third of White and Hispanic teens, along with two-fifths of Black teens, say they are likely to continue to attend a Christian church in the near future, when they are living independent of their parents.

With an aging demographic yet growing population of African Americans from varying parts of the Diaspora, it makes sense to be growing leaders that will be equipped to handle the mantle of leadership when the time comes. I contend that missional leadership can be attained "in North American black and Hispanic churches where a strong family structure" still exists. Many have not followed the North American trends as closely and their pattern of leadership and church based-operation was still largely in place.

At the same time there has been significant growth among minority groups. The [Church] community in North America is on the threshold of a "majority minority" situation in which none of the four major ethnic segments will constitute a majority.

Because music has always been a part of my life, I would dare to say that music is also a part of your life. It accompanies you when you go shopping. There is music that goes with you when you travel. Even if you're a person who is not that into music, you cannot escape its influence in the media you take in. The church is not exempt from music's influence. As a matter of fact, my ideas about restoration of leadership are influenced by my experiences in music at my most formative years. I think this may be yours too. And if it's not, we'll work together through the chapters of this book to restore the music that's missing. It is a restoring of young leaders prepared from an early age to take the reins of leadership in the local church. I believe the music of this restoration is similar to the work songs of the slave, or even the gospel music of the church. There is a music that is the leadership of young adults, that when captured, will positively affect the culture of leadership in the Church. The music will keep us moving forward.

Chapter 1
A LITTLE MUSIC HISTORY

Before anyone ever gets to sing a song in church, they have to learn about the music. Sometimes we learn about the artist, or the writer and their motivations. When we sing or perform the music, it becomes ours. It's a little different because of the nuances that we bring to the performance. Our experiences and culture influence how we perform the music. In this section, I will do a review of Adventist literature on the formation of youth ministry in the Adventist church in general, to learn about the history of youth and young adult ministry. I will be searching for possible trends that are born out of past research and attempting to identify if there are additional research areas that can be mined from the available literature. By no means is this an exhaustive review, but one that will be reviewed repeatedly over the course of our study.

Missing chords

When there are chords missing in a piece of music, we will notice spaces where music should go. We should hear continuous streams, but now we hear music in stops and starts. These missing chords are the vital and sometimes forgotten young adults of the local church. Before *UnChristian* was making the rounds of the evangelical circuit, the Adventist church embarked on a daunting 10-year study called Valuegenesis[1].

1 Brantley, Paul S. 1993. [Valuegenesis study of Seventh-Day Adventist

From this research came a book based on the study authored by Roger Dudley, *Why Our Teenagers Leave the Church*. Using the stories from 1,500 Adventist young people he determined that there are some factors that are causing our youth and young adults to walk away from the Adventist church and in many instances, from faith altogether. Most aren't leaving the church because of a dispute with doctrine but are confused by the tension between the truth of Adventism and the way they see it lived out by the older members of their congregations.[2]

What was discovered through a diligent review of the survey responses was a number of themes that dominate the answers given:

- **Alienation** – they feel unaccepted by their churches; some felt as if they were not needed or valued by their churches.

- **Irrelevance** – They perceive the church as either not interested or simply clueless to their generation's needs.

- **Intolerance** – A common theme among many of the dropouts involves sensitivity to and distaste for the intolerant attitudes they perceive in the church. A number feel very uncomfortable with the image they see their church projecting as the only true church, that is "holier than thou."

- **Convenience** – the church was not convenient for those who lived fast-paced lives. A number expressed their urge to recoup and sleep in on Sabbath mornings.

- **Minor themes** – Premarital pregnancy resulting in the church asking them to leave; interpersonal conflicts; others revealed they were in a stage of rebellion and experimentation because of the strictness of their upbringing.

---

youth]. *JRCE* 2 (1):81-118.

2 Dudley, Roger L. 2000. *Why our teenagers leave the church: personal stories from a 10-year study*. Hagerstown, MD: Review and Herald Pub. Association.

The work done in *UnChristian* mirrors some of these themes, but not to find out why young people leave, but why those on the outside of the Christian faith (those termed outsiders in the book) are not willing to come in. There is an interesting juxtaposition that takes place looking at these two books. Both look at youth and young adult attitudes toward church. Dudley's looking at SDA's specifically, while Kinnaman looks at those who claim anything but Christianity for the most part. Kinnaman deals with two generations (Busters and Mosaics) while Dudley's work follows the Busters primarily.

As we continue to seek out research on this demographic, any information that we can gain from the Center for Creative Ministry (An Adventist Research group) will prove important. It is possible that my research can spark something that can be made national or even church wide.

Summary

Although there is a documented exodus of the young adult populations of many SDA churches, there are some who stay. The local church should invest time and energy developing the "ships" in youth ministry and acknowledging the needs of young adults in their congregations. Because of changes in time and culture, an updated theology for youth and young adult ministry has been adopted. This theology is all about the kingdom of God. The youth and young adult ministry for the Seventh-day Adventist church is supposed to prepare, present, and participate in the kingdom of God. This new, or updated paradigm still must contend with the existing challenges to developing leaders in our churches. Research and continual dialogue among scholars can assist in developing models that can assist in leadership growth.

Chapter 2

WHAT HAS LEADERSHIP SOUNDED LIKE?

Now let's look at the people we want to make the music. We're now looking at what are the factors that will allow young adults to participate in the music of leadership. What do various sources say about youth, young adults, and leadership in general, then reviewing urban leadership specifically.

Music isn't born, it's made

In the large amounts of youth ministry material available, urban youth leadership is not a singular topic. Not much on the development of youth and young adults, but a wealth of information on leading youth and young adults in ministry. The reason for this is that the urban young adults do not exist. In most instances, authors are writing to prepare someone who already may be in ministry or for volunteers that would be assisting at the local church level. Books such as *Raising Up Young Heroes, Grace Based Youth Ministry, Black Young Adults: How to Reach Them, What to Teach Them,* and *Hip-Hop Church* frame the discussion on inner-city youth leadership. There are no manuals on how to reproduce leadership, there are smatterings of articles that are in denominational specific magazines. I propose that there is a rubric that can be used across cultures, although our research is specific to African American young adults.

There are specific outcomes that are expected within each

urban youth ministry paradigm:

- To stir the consciousness of African Americans as to the importance of discipling and evangelizing youth and college students
- To challenge adults to disciple biblically
- To suggest that we put performance indicators in place
- To evaluate our efforts
- To offer resources to aid in discipling and evangelizing[3]

In the earliest parts of the 20th century, there was a desire to see our young adults take active leadership. One of the greatest needs of the church is a consecrated and intelligent lay leadership . . .we have a right to expect that college graduates will assume large leadership in the churches to which they belong, and that the Christian colleges and the Christian programs in connection with state universities shall prepare them specifically for this task[4].

Ministry to this group and those of their demographic was to include:

- A presentation of religion from the pulpit that gives young people a clear understanding of the meaning of Christianity.
- An experience of worship that feeds the inner life, so that the propelling power of Christianity will move them to a selfless expression of the gospel of Jesus in church and community life after college.

---

[3] Copeland, Nelson E. 1995. *The heroic revolution: a new agenda for urban youthwork*. Nashville, TN: J.C. Winston.

[4] Stock, Harry Thomas, and Erwin L. Shaver. 1933. *Young people and their leaders*. Boston; Chicago; Printed for the Leadership Training Pub. association by the Pilgrim Press.

- A program of service on behalf of social righteousness which will send these students into adult responsibilities committed to the high purposes of Jesus Christ and will make them restless and intelligent disciples of the Master, imparting His convictions and quality of life to children and youth.

- A fellowship with other Christians that raises the church as an institution through which the gospel of Jesus will be meditated upon

Stock and Shaver document what youth leadership was in the context of denominational and interdenominational groups training young people through the Christian education system, identifying ways in which leadership can be transferred, taught, and caught. Good leadership just doesn't happen. It has to be cultivated and developed. The church seriously working at youth ministry will be working at developing leadership skills among youth.[5]

When wanting to continue the music of leadership we must be cognizant of the developmental stages of young people. The following model used in the United Methodist Church takes these changes into account. In the Leadership transfer model, we see an increased level of responsibility being placed on the youth as they pass through phases of adolescence.

---

5 Courtoy, Charles, and Clifford E. Kolb. 1971. *Organizing for youth ministry* of *Basic leadership series*. Nashville: Division of the Local Church Board of Education of The United Methodist Church.

Leadership transfer model

Early Teens	Middle Teens	Late Teens
	Intellectual and psychological growth	
Selected tasks under guidance of adult leaders	Increased ability in planning and implementing plans with adult support and some guidance	Ability to plan and implement plans with adults supporting

In addition to the above model for ministry, the most important aspect to share with young believers is <u>koinonia</u>. Koinonia is the Greek word that means Christian fellowship or communion with God or more commonly, with fellow Christians. The church is supposed to be a community of acceptance, ministry, and corporate action. But no adult can help a young person enter into a caring, covenanting community, unless he or she is a part of a caring, covenanting community, also. [6]

Many of our youth groups, clubs, and para-church ministries have done events well, but not excelled in community building. Young people naturally gravitate to the charismatic and outgoing leader, who has the awesome programs and music, but leave not having grown in their character or developing their leadership traits. Other times they grow up in the youth group, have fun, but are never encouraged to lead in any other aspect of church ministry. Some suggest that this can be achieved through mission trips. Although that is not the focus of this study, the idea of leadership development through the use of mission trips specifically for urban youth is intriguing and can be further researched in post-doctorate work. My study is specific to the local church and its role in the

---

6 Ng, David. 1984. *Youth in the community of disciples*. Valley Forge, PA: Judson Press.

development of young adult leaders.

The key to a youth ministry that actively moves on the Word of God is to have an environment in which leadership from young people is affirmed. Youth leaders may say they want youth to take leadership, but when they see it in action they often have a different feeling.[7] It will always feel uncomfortable to know that there is supposed to be someone to take your place, but that is the circle of life, to borrow a phrase from "The Lion King." What we should be striving for in youth and young adult ministries is not a circle of life, but a circle of leaders.

The music of leadership hasn't been continually playing because present leadership hasn't been willing to teach the music to their successors. Existing leaders must not only acknowledge the presence of potential leaders but use their capital within the church to hand over "the keys of leadership."[8] I have been fortunate to be able to hand off leadership to young men and women in whom I saw leadership potential. Some were willing, and others not so willing. The key was that I told them I was available to them for all their questions to be answered, and that I wanted to see them do a better job than I did. May the circle be unbroken!

What my experience has shown me in the past 14+ years in youth ministry is that youth leaders tend not to look for their replacement, but someone who can make their load a little lighter. Then by default, there may be a transfer of leadership, whether by the leader moving on but at no time was there a formal transfer. Now you have a new leader in a position they were never really prepared for. As a result, their tenure in the position will be limited barring someone pouring into them as a mentor. More on that later.

---

7   Smith, Efrem. 2004. *Raising up young heroes: developing a revolutionary youth ministry*. Downers Grove, Ill.: InterVarsity Press.
8   Clark, Chap, and Kara Eckmann Powell. 2007. *Deep justice in a broken world: helping your kids serve others and right the wrongs around them*. Grand Rapids, MI El Cajon, CA: Zondervan; Youth Specialties.

How the music used to sound

The music of youth leadership in the African American church used to be continuous and robust. Much of the socialization for children and youth occurs through the process of role modeling – observing, evaluating, emulating, and filing away for later use the behavioral examples, and values of others.[9] This spiritual and cultural reservoir was filled with the experiences of African Americans through slavery, Reconstruction, the Depression, and the civil rights movement. This music felt throughout Black Churches historically has always highlighted the desire for freedom. Freedom from oppression, freedom from poverty. Freedom from inequality. Freedom from being held down, held back, and held in check. Young people desire the same freedoms today. In the chapter, Forging Freedom, in the book *Youth Ministry in Modern America: 1930 to the Present*, a historical timeline is created through the models of four types of youth ministries.

Bethel A.M.E Church

The youth ministry at the Bethel A.M.E. Church, Baltimore Maryland was the headquarters for the City-Wide Young People's Forum:

This agency, led by Juanita Jackson, who eventually became youth director for the NAACP, sponsored programs to "develop the intellectual and moral talents" of young African Americans …Along with members of the National Urban League, Bethel's youth "picketed and boycotted the city's chain stores, which refused to hire Negro clerks. They also protested segregation at the Enoch Pratt Public Library, and held mass meetings to demonstrate against" two Maryland lynching's in 1932 and 1933… Through such meetings, and through Sunday sermons and Scripture readings, young black Christians learned and practiced liberation theology at Bethel A.M.E. Church well before it was given a name as a movement within Christian theology.[10]

---

9   Lincoln, C. Eric, and Lawrence H. Mamiya. 1990. *The Black church in the African-American experience*. Durham: Duke University Press.
10 Pahl, Jon. 2000. *Youth ministry in modern America: 1930 to the present.*

In subsequent years, Bethel's youth would also be involved in what would be termed traditional youth ministry activities, such as Bible study, prayer, and singing. During the 50's and the 60's the young people of Bethel were called on to engage in a number of events; even the most "innocuous events held social significance". The young women were taught the value of their bodies by being enlisted in a fashion show. This was seen as a "significant cultural and theological affirmation." Bethel's youth were also taught about economic empowerment, desegregation, civil rights activism, and "that the life-path of freedom had practical as well as spiritual benefits."

Bethel's youth ministry from 1930 to 1970 showcased an active youth group led by adults who cared. They were taught to value their freedom and to "apply it from a community to which they feel connected" to change the world.

Where Bethel excelled in getting its young people on the life-path to freedom through civic activity, Grace Church sought freedom for its youth by establishing a place where they felt belonging, worship and the ability to be cultural critics.

Grace Church

The youth ministry of Grace Church, a Midwestern middle-class, an urban African American church employed the kinship model of youth ministry. From the out of print *Black and White Styles of Youth Ministry* by Seminary Professor William Myers, the Kinship Model centers on intergenerational, communal worship, and the empowerment of adolescents who can critique mainstream culture from a theological, African American stance.[11]

The corporate model of youth ministry normally has a youth pastor hired to run what many might call a 'separate church'. This type of youth ministry can create an 'us vs. them' type of feeling. It can also

Peabody, Mass.: Hendrickson Publishers.
11 Pahl, Jon. 2000. *Youth ministry in modern America: 1930 to the present.* Peabody, Mass.: Hendrickson Publishers.

cause division within the church as young people seek to 'have their own' as opposed to contributing to the whole.

At the center of the kinship model of youth ministry at Grace has been the intentional involving of the young people in the worship life of the church. The pastor has read the report cards of young congregants from the pulpit, young people regularly read the lessons, and at least once a month, during Youth Sunday, youth have preached. [12]

"It takes a whole village to raise a child."[13] The truth and depth of this simple phrase has become a rallying cry for those concerned with the educational, spiritual, moral, and social needs of American children.[14]

Since the sixties Grace church has sought the salvation of their youth not through civic and community endeavors, but through an intentional upholding of the African communal concepts married to keeping the youth engaged in worship. This is exemplified in its credo to be both "unashamedly black" and "unapologetically Christian."

Building Educational Strategies for Teens (BEST)

The history of urban youth ministry is most notably rooted in the African American church, but is that the only place where young people can find rest, or sanctuary? Historically, the lines between sacred and secular have been fluid in African American communities. Some churches have gone the road less travelled and sought to partner with community and begin nonprofit agencies. These urban sanctuaries have sought to be respites for youth with no spiritual strings attached. One such agency is BEST – Building Educational Strategies for Teens.

BEST began in 1965 as a special youth ministry program for a

---

12 Ibid.
13 Igbo and Yoruba (Nigeria) Proverb
14 Dunn, Richard R., and Mark Senter. 1997. *Reaching a generation for Christ: a comprehensive guide to youth ministry*. Chicago: Moody Press.

congregation situated in a heavily African American section of a Midwestern city. It began as a non-profit organization that received funding from the church initially, but now receives funds from a broad-based network of grassroots, corporate, governmental, foundation, and individual donors. BEST provides a sanctuary for inner-city young people.[15]

Everyday life at BEST in many ways resembles the typical family as many Americans imagine it. Youngsters come in after school, get themselves a snack (from the machines in the entry hall), do their homework at tables with their "brothers and sisters." They take breaks to play games or work on special projects, and occasionally settle down with staff or other members to talk about long-range plans for a Saturday visit to the museum, the zoo, a big game or even for college or travel. While focused as an educational program, BEST provides both personal and academic resources as well as broadening experiences for the children and youth who come to the afterschool activities and to summer day camp.

BEST employed what is described in the next chapter as the "safe place" model. Within our four types of youth ministry (traditional, corporate, kinship, safe place), these three historical models (Bethel, Grace, BEST) of African American youth ministry exemplify what is generally seen in the Black Church. There is either a strong emphasis on civic duty of the African American youth to be involved in the community because of the many ills of society seem to affect those of African descent disproportionately to the dominant culture, or a strong emphasis on what is termed 'in-reach' preparing the existing youth base to learn how to function within the church paradigm ultimately preparing them for life.

All the churches within my study have ministries dedicated to community service. These departments don't define the ethos of the individual churches, but they are an active arm, very active in some cases, of the ministry of the church. Every community service

---

15 Pahl, Jon. 2000. *Youth ministry in modern America: 1930 to the present.* Peabody, Mass.: Hendrickson Publishers.

department is entrusted with the task of defining how the church can serve the community and what kind of community resource the church can become. In trying to live out the Salvation and Service credo of [our] youth ministry, there needs to be a facility to marry both civic action and in-reach. Is there room to teach missional values within the culture of the already existing ministry, or should we concentrate on building something else?

In the past, we've seen success in youth ministry coincide with a young people being active in the community endeavors and standing for justice. Today we find a push for justice in some places and curriculum based on Deep Justice.[16] Can the music of youth leadership hinge on how active a youth group is in their community? In a culture of Millennials who want to leave their mark on the world, is it possible that the leadership of young people in the church can be correlated to how active these same young people are outside of it?

The robust music of youth and young adult leadership of the past was propelled by the drumbeat of activism and community involvement. What has stopped the music of leadership today?

What's stopping the music?

No matter the type of music in your ministry, there are a myriad of factors that stop the music of leadership from playing consistently. Churches are held up by the start and stop of pastoral leadership, among other distractions. According to *Youth Ministry in City Churches*, there are four overarching barriers (or music stoppers):

- **Churches lack motivation** – because of the energy and time commitment that is necessary to win urban youth, a church that is not passionate about seeing youth and young adults won to Christ is in danger of falling into a malaise of doing the same things, getting the same results, then criticizing the culture of

---

16 Clark, Chap, and Kara Eckmann Powell. 2007. *Deep justice in a broken world: helping your kids serve others and right the wrongs around them.* Grand Rapids, MI. El Cajon, CA: Zondervan; Youth Specialties.

young people for not coming to the Church. Feelings of failure keep many churches from being consistent in their outreach to urban youth and young adults.

- **Teenagers don't feel comfortable** – when teenagers don't feel comfortable they may be apathetic to Church. When they are not comfortable as teenagers, they become young adults who are nomads,[17] they walk away from church engagement but still consider themselves Christian.

- **Common youth ministry models don't apply** – what works in homogenous settings doesn't always work or translate properly in the urban settings. Lack of properly trained youth/young adult leaders attempting to use one-size-fits-most youth ministry models realize that they need to seek out more creative models that fit in the urban context.

- **Few quality resources available** – there are not as many authors/pastors/teachers writing about how to not only practice youth/young adult ministry in decidedly urban contexts, and among those, even fewer writing about leadership development for young adults in the local church.

In Black churches and communities of color the prevailing challenge is that of the underclass. This segment of the black populace is said to "make up one third of all black families".[18] Other challenges that are specific to African Americans and those in the inner city include 1) the rise of the unchurched population; 2) the ambivalence of racial identity; and 3) an increase in the number of blacks (males in particular) that are incarcerated.

Among the four-basic youth ministry life-paths promoted by

---

17 Kinnaman, David, and Gabe Lyons. 2007. *Unchristian: what a new generation really thinks about Christianity-- and why it matters*. Grand Rapids, Mich.: Baker Books.
18 Lincoln, C. Eric, and Lawrence H. Mamiya. 1990. *The Black church in the African-American experience*. Durham: Duke University Press.

Pahl, these are the barriers or common problems:

1. **The problem of private and public theologies.** The power of "civic faith" to disrupt, if not destroy, authentic Christian faith among youth. The private faiths of African Americans were susceptible to the corrosive power of modern marketed culture, on the one hand and the hegemonic power of the state on the other. All four historical settings of youth ministry demonstrated leaders and youth alike struggling to identify the appropriate intersections and interpenetrations of the private faiths of Christians and the public possibilities of American culture. For African Americans this problem crystallized over the issue of violence. The violence facing African Americans was immediate and closer to home. That these youth were being asked to die for freedoms abroad that they did not experience at home occurred to more than one African American observer. So, they took that fact to the streets with them to struggle nonviolently to turn their private faith into public law. In today's day and age, the marketed culture is one that is glorified in the media of young men as hustler's and pimps, while young ladies have to war against the urban stereotypes of loose living exemplified in provocative and suggestive clothing. The hip hop culture, while varied in its forms, is one major vehicle that the media now employs to sell a lifestyle that is incongruous to that of the church-going young adult.

2. **The problem of volunteer programs.** The fact that they were all "volunteer programs." It was the will of the youth to participate. They were programs. For the African American youth, the choices available to middle-class youth multiplied, while the need for choices among the urban underclass intensified.

3. **The problem of becoming and belonging.** The rise of youth ministry is, on one level, a response to adolescent flight and a strategy to enlist belonging. The "four" (traditional, corporate,

kinship, civic/kinship hybrid or safe place) were rarely so upfront about their purpose, and in many ways, they also contributed to the general cultural understanding of adolescence as a time of becoming. African Americans held the tension together best, conjuring Christianity by becoming Christians but belonging to a community of people who also asserted that they belonged to more than just America. In the Black church, however, young adults are increasingly finding other avenues of becoming and belonging more attractive than churches. These groups can be defined by what they have in common, or who they consistently spend time with. They are termed exiles. They are still invested in their Christian faith but feel stuck (or lost) between culture and the church.

4. **From purity to practices.** The Christian life demands such a movement from purity to practices; the gospel stories of Jesus' life are rendered moot without it. The move is not easy. African Americans have kept pace best-both drawing upon the depths of conjuring Christianity and dressing the message in the idioms and styles of modernity. In any case, the movements came closest to each other when they were truest to their own visions while also attending mindfully to the realities of modern America.

In short, we see that the "common" problems that existed in general with youth ministry take particularly potent and different nuances when placed in the context of African American culture in America. Lincoln and Mamiya's barriers take into account the incarcerated, which continues to be a problem in this country today. These other themes contrast in a way with Roehlkepartain, who is specifically writing about city churches. He struggles with not wanting to offend in his terminology claiming, "the word 'urban,' for example, carries with it a great deal of baggage. Even more sensitive is the issue of identifying various groups of people, whether by income or by racial or ethnic background."[19]

---

19 Roehlkepartain, Eugene C. 1989. *Youth ministry in city churches*. Loveland, Colo.: Group Books.

Summary

The music of youth ministry within the African American church in the US has always provided leadership development in the context of civic activity. Where civic activity has diminished, in urban areas, the church has not been able to successfully fill the void. There are definite issues to be overcome within the urban African American Church as it relates to youth ministry. Moreover, within the Adventist church these same realities abound. Yet there is not much scholarship to prove, refute, or lead the conversation in another direction; one more reason to be involved in the research of African American youth leadership. The Christian education system was the place where leadership could be transferred, taught and caught.

Chapter 3

THE MUSIC OF YOUTH AND YOUNG ADULT MINISTRY

The music of youth and young adult ministry has many variations, just like the music in a music store. Also, I will talk about existing doors of access to young adults in San Bernardino. Here we will list and describe the models that encompass the breadth of youth ministry in the U.S. since models were first identified in Youth Education in the Church.

A. Christian school model builds young people into well rounded Christian adults using the Christian high school as a social, academic, and spiritual laboratory, shaped by Christian worldview, so as adults the graduates will live as Christians in a non-Christian world.

B. The competition model uses natural leaders from the high school society, trained to serve as servants and motivators to their teams in the context of team competition, to attract and hold high students for an articulate confrontation with biblical truth, both in a large group setting and in smaller discipleship groups.

C. The discipleship model trains students to be God's people in an ungodly world, equipped with Bible study and prayer skills developed in a caring atmosphere with a view to reproducing their Christian lives in others.

D. The ministry model develops student ministry skills and a context in which to use those skills through carefully planned exposure to human and spiritual needs outside the cultural context of the church, enhanced through meeting similar needs in the community surrounding the church and supported by accountability groups within the youth group.

E. The safe place model uses the equipment and facilities of the church or youth center in conjunction with the presence of loving Christian adults who have earned the right to be heard in the world of the students who are at risk. Those adults then have the opportunity to reach the kids and build spiritually accountable relationships with them. The context is a sustained contact with mature Christians at a local church or youth center.[20]

Despite the fact that there are specific models of traditional youth ministry, more often than not, it is not as clear cut. Depending on whether there is a strong Youth Leader or Youth Pastor, many ministries blend elements from 2 or more of the models available as the needs arise. Models "A" and "B" only exist within churches that have church schools or academies attached to them. Models "C", "D", and "E" are almost interchangeable depending on the program of the week for the youth.

With the basic models outlined, there are still some other models that are emerging. Senter continues with the following submissions: family-based youth ministry, the high school subpopulation model, the meta model, and Youth church model.

A. In the family based model, parents, aided by their faith communities, guide their children to intellectual, emotional,

---

[20] Dunn, Richard R., and Mark Senter. 1997. *Reaching a generation for Christ: a comprehensive guide to youth ministry*. Chicago: Moody Press.

social, moral, and spiritual maturity while using their distinctive giftedness to witness to the broader community of adolescents and their families.

In the high school subpopulation model, Christian adults with similar interests or backgrounds to youth within specific subpopulations of adolescent society discover a means by which to build relationships with that group of people and share both a love for the common interest and a love for Jesus Christ. The desire is to elicit an interest in spiritual matters that might lead the young person to faith in Jesus Christ and participation in the believing community.

B. In the meta model, adult and student leaders equip and empower caring Christian cell groups to multiply in amoeba-like fashion in order to create an expanding network of friendship clusters in which students share their lives with each other and discuss the life of Christ with spiritually open peers.

C. In the youth church model, the youth minister and spiritually gifted and qualified adults prepare young people to be spiritual leaders by taking responsibility to establish a new church either within an existing church, as a spin-off of a church that seeks to plant a new church. It could be the logical outcome of the ministry of a para-church organization.

Youth Ministry Top Ten

The music of youth and young adult ministry can take on the different forms similar to different styles of music. The following are models of ministry that are the most frequently seen in the local church context. This is not an exhaustive list, and we will revisit this list later in the text. This list also is not in order of importance or frequency.

1. **The Lost and Found Model** – believes that every human being is lost, and that God seeks to find every lost person. This model incorporates all of the community's gifts of faith to reach those who are lost. Celebrations for every found person and sadness for every lost one causes this model to function like a roller coaster. It can create an "us" versus "them" type of atmosphere.

2. **The Wholistic Worship Model** – all of life can be found in worship to God. God doesn't just show up at church but is present in all mundane activities. An awareness of holy ground impacts how we treat others at all times and in every situation.

3. **The Discipleship Model** – Discipleship is a journey. And as such it requires that we come alongside others, teaching, listening, growing, communicating, and learning. People act as models for mentees. Discipleship finds its root in discipline. Learning spiritual practices, as well as choosing and planning for growth.

4. **The Family Based Model** – Congregations empower families to provide religious instruction, worship experiences, service activities, and social interaction rather than separating for age specific programming. Creates a positive family dynamic for those who may not experience one naturally.

5. **The Missional Model** – Based on the Gospel Commission and the promise from God to equip His people to fulfill it, this model expects and encourages youth and young adults to share the gospel – now.

6. **The Social Advocacy Model** – this moves from short-term acts of service to embrace justice. This requires an entrance into the world of the marginalized, living with them, and changing the systems that keep them marginalized.

7. **The Small Groups Model** – this model stands in contrast to the idea of "bigger is better." Small groups are developed for personal and spiritual growth.

8. **The Cross-Cultural Model** – this model focuses on bringing diverse people together in following Jesus. It follows a set of A-D's:
    i. Awareness of Differences
    ii. Acceptance of Diversity
    iii. Agreement on Direction
    iv. Application of Design

9. **The Relational Model** – sometimes referred to as the friendship or "warm, fuzzy model", this model gives priority to relationships. Certain personalities do this naturally, but not always with a purpose. This model desires for its adherents to meet others on purpose.

10. **The Leadership Model** – empowers youth and young adults by developing them as ministry leaders. Inherent in this model is the expectation that young people can lead and do so now.

The models presented from the Symposium are supposed to be models that have been tried and known to be successful. Unfortunately, the best we can see is that these are still theories with the anecdotal evidence of the practitioners who presented them. This leadership model holds some interest for me as we are looking for the models that have an outcome of leadership development. This model can prove to be useful in our designing a leadership transfer model for San Bernardino young adults. We will revisit these 10 in light of my findings in a later chapter.

Urban youth ministry models

Revisiting the safe place model of youth ministry as one that is typically found in urban settings, there are some other possible sub-categories outlined in other literature. In *The Heroic Revolution*, Copeland espouses a four-pronged approach to his new agenda for youth ministry.

- **The primacy of salvation for teens** – the highest goal of every

Christian youth group is the conversion of its teenagers to Christianity.

- **The primacy of evangelism from the teens** – One of the most significant things any youth pastor can do is involve youth in evangelism. City youth will often know of contextual ways to preach to their peers that may go far beyond what the youth pastor can understand.

- **The primacy of social action from the teens** – Teenagers must participate in the ongoing world of God. Social action, like evangelism, must be performed by the teens themselves. Young people are never the same after they allow God to work through them.

- **The primacy of empowering teens** – Teenagers from the city feel they have no power over their destiny. Urban youth need opportunities for ownership in their neighborhoods and youth groups, which may translate into sending teams of adolescents to community meetings, so they can know and respond to the decisions being made over them or giving more leadership to youth in the local youth group.[21]

In *Hip-Hop Church*, Smith and Jackson promote the Youth church model since "the church can't avoid the cultural context that young people live in. The church cannot avoid the culture that now has global and intergenerational influence. The church cannot avoid the culture of the un-churched postmodern urban community. To avoid hip-hop, given its wide influence on young people, is in some ways avoiding the youth themselves and treating them as modern-day Samaritans."[22]

Emerging hip-hop ministry churches in Queens, New York (New Life Fellowship), Tampa, Florida (Crossover Church), and Chicago, Illinois (Da House @ Lawndale Community Church) illustrate how

---

21 Copeland, Nelson E. 1995. *The heroic revolution: a new agenda for urban youthwork*. Nashville, TN: J.C. Winston.
22 Smith, Efrem, and Phil Jackson. 2005. *The hip-hop church: connecting with the movement shaping our culture*. Downers Grove, Ill.: InterVarsity Press.

to put the Safe place and Youth church models into practice. The challenge with this model and with these worship settings is that they many times do not reach others outside the culture or age group. Even when there is a facility for leadership training, it will not be well rounded or intergenerational.

Within this urban youth church model Smith and Jackson assert that there are things that the Church in general and the African American church in particular, must wrestle with: in this post-soul culture there is a widening gap between African American culture and the church. Further, there is a widening gap between the urban church and its surrounding community.[23]

In complement to Senter, Fernando Arzola, Jr. outlines four paradigms of youth ministry in the urban context:

I. **The traditional youth ministry paradigm** – a program-centric model. This is the most common in the urban context. The emphasis in this paradigm is on youth ministry in the urban context. For the traditional youth ministry, the root principle is discipleship, to become disciples of Christ. At its best, the traditional youth ministry challenges us to be rooted in the life and teaching of Jesus Christ. At its worst, it is more concerned with winning souls, indoctrination into a specific tradition and engaging in spiritual warfare at the expense of addressing the social injustices of this world.

II. **The liberal youth ministry paradigm** – very popular with mainline denominational churches, particularly within middle-class and upper-middle-class neighborhoods. The emphasis of this paradigm is on compassionate ministry for urban youth. The liberal paradigm is based on an ideology of evolution. That is, youth ministries need to change and adapt. Therefore, the liberal paradigm believes that youth ministry as an institution, needs to be reformed.

---

23 Ibid.

III. **The activist youth ministry paradigm** – The emphasis is on urban ministry for youth. That is, its primary purpose is developing an urban ministry centered program for youth. At its best, the activist paradigm challenges us to be engaged in addressing systematic injustice and social sin. At its worst, it can be overly concerned with deconstructing traditions, fighting systems and overturning institutions rather than growing in Christ.

IV. **The prophetic youth paradigm** – the youth ministry paradigm used the least. The emphasis of this ministry is Christian ministry for urban youth. That is, its primary purpose is developing a Christ-centered ministry for urban youth.

Reviewing these models and then thinking through my own experience in youth ministry over the years, I find that with the exception of the Christian education model, I have tried some aspect of each. The Leadership Transfer Model seems to be what many would traditionally see in the Black church as part of the Rites of Passage programs and the like. Leaders are not always trained as part of a rigid process, but ministry can go up and down based on whoever the youth leader is. Within the Black Adventist church having a Youth Pastor is a luxury, not a right. Nor is it expected all the time. In lieu of the Youth Pastor, there is the AY (Adventist Youth) leader. This leader is usually a volunteer voted on by the church at large. Many times, these volunteers don't get the training that they need, and seldom are they assessed for their ability to lead. As a result, we watch youth groups ebb and flow with the personality and time constraints of the leader.

Within Arzola's description of urban youth ministry models, we find that Senter's descriptions can be folded in with overlap in some areas. Where traditional youth ministry is in the urban setting, we have the discipleship and ministry models. For the liberal model in Arzola's description, there is the meta model from Senter's newer paradigms, and so on and so on. There is no equal from one model to the next, but there are perspectives that parallel one another. Whether the outcome is for discipleship or for youth involvement in the community, we have a model of youth ministry for it. The question remains what is the model that is best suited for the urban African American youth/young adult to be led into, or prepared for leadership at the local level and ultimately in the greater world community?

Chapter 4

CAN YOU HEAR ME NOW?

The attitudes of young adults toward leadership are impacted by the awareness of their pastors to involve them early. In churches where a youth pastor is present, the involvement of young adults is significantly higher. The challenge for the local pastor and the youth pastor is that in attempting to meet the spiritual needs of the young people they serve, they don't always know when to begin leadership training. Among the youth pastor's I surveyed, there were different ages and stages of life. None wanted to start too early as to burn out the young people, and all believed it could be too late if they waited until college. As a result, we have youth pastors wanting to see more young adults involved but have no procedural way to do it.

It's kind of like that friend who has that song that they really like, and they think you should like it also, but you don't. Yet every time they see you or you're in their space that song comes on. You look at them and say, "I'm not feeling it." Music is so subjective, and the way young adults interpret music is as well. You can remember growing up listening to the songs of your parents. While you may have thought it was okay, you made completely different music choices for yourself. I came up at a time when identity was important, so I gravitated to the songs of my culture while hip-hop was being developed in the streets. African American young people view leadership in much the same way. They want to appreciate what came before and be free to make their own choices as to how they will lead in the future, if they ever decide to lead.

There are a few themes that emerge from our interviews and focus groups as to why young adults were avoiding leadership. Chief among them was the lack of young adults in the churches surveyed. Even the group that had the largest representation, there was a desire for more young adults in leadership or just present at their church. Another repeating theme was a lack of consistent leadership from the pastoral standpoint. Traditionally, it used to be that senior pastors in the African American churches have an average tenure of three to four years. Here in Southern California, it's closer to five years. At the time of this research, changes in pastoral leadership left a few churches without pastors while the Conference sought to fill the open positions. The last of the most repeated themes was a challenge with church members and leadership in some places that is not willing to change or change fast enough for the young adults in their midst. In the end, what we found is the attitudes of African American young adults toward leadership are impacted mainly by the lack of the peer group in the churches, inconsistent leaders, and frustration with a system that is unwilling to change.

Reasons for lack of involvement

Pressure

In the case of young adults who are active and involved, even though they are not in leadership, they feel the pressure of expectations in leadership that they cannot live up to or at least don't think they can live up to. One young adult called it a 'spirit of competition' where he thought it's "tough to lead in this environment." They feel pressure to perform. This pressure of expectation is doubly egregious when dealing with a population who is already uncomfortable with their "new adulthood" and are now being pushed toward responsibility without being adequately trained (in their opinion). When young adults are unsure, there are feelings like those expressed by a young lady who is active at her church, "It's nerve racking to lead (do things)" as a result she is not always willing.

Fear

Young adults in transition have a fear of failure and as a result eschew leadership opportunities. Even if they were involved as teens, there is no guarantee that they will continue in any ministry of the church without help. Many fear what the church will think about them. I asked all the young adults in the focus groups if they were affirmed at their home churches. They all responded and gave examples of affirmation; they all were not confident or comfortable with accepting leadership roles. Among those who did participate in the worship services on some level, the fear was not only of failure, but a fear of becoming like a parent who may give "too much" to the church. They have not seen healthy relationships or leaders in the church and fear they may be repeating a cycle they saw come before them. As a result, they don't bother.

Lack of mentorship

A few of the young adults mentioned the need for mentorship at the local church level. One young lady said,

> "I think the shadowing aspect, you know how they do in regular jobs, they (church members) don't really show you how to do it. They're like "hey can you do this for me", like there! Do it how you think it should be done, Nah, let me take you through the process, or this is what you could say or if you need help let me know, contact me. There really isn't that helping aspect." – SB2

This lack of mentorship also contributes to the chasm between the generations. The young adults think it's the job of the elderly and the baby boomers to train the young adults, but they have not received it. One young man said, "There is a whole lot of talking, but not a lot of helping." There were, however, two positive mentoring relationships that were explained in the groups. One was of a young adult who taught the young men of the church how to run the Audiovisual equipment. Once the young men were proficient, he charged them to teach other young people as they got older. Another was the mentoring of a young man at one of the local churches. The senior pastor saw the gifts this young man displayed and assigned him a mentor. This young man now serves as a pastoral intern in the church where he grew up. Unfortunately, these stories are the exception, not the rule.

In areas where mentoring is lacking from the top down, perhaps it is time to look into reverse mentoring.[24] This would not only address the mentoring gap by changing the mindset of the older leaders, but that also of the young leaders by following a system of teaching up.

Lack of peer group

When I was growing up, I would hear the phrase "a crowd creates a crowd" and "like attracts like." These same themes are applicable in today's church climate. African American young adults want to go to places where they see people who are or are around their age. One responder said, "not having young adults at church causes less young people to come to church." Another in the SB1 group vehemently declared that he knew at least 15 people on his campus who were former Adventists but left to go to other denominations because they had larger numbers within their peer group.

Teaching young adults how to win their friends to Christ in non-threatening ways could go a long way to addressing this issue. Among the respondents' ideas like "youth to youth" and "the younger the leader the more willing (young people are) to listen. One respondent went so far as to suggest "inception," the concept of placing an idea in the mind of a young adult for them to reach out

---

24 Creps, Earl G. 2008. *Reverse mentoring: how young leaders can transform the church and why we should let them.* 1st ed. San Francisco, CA: Jossey-Bass.

to their sphere of influence.

Lack of connection

Many of the young adults in my focus groups have spent at least half of their lives at the church they currently attend. The members of their congregations have affirmed them all at one time or another, yet, they do not feel connected to them. They see their churches as places that are not welcoming. They feel like they cannot be themselves at their churches. They believe, in some instances, that they are no different than the visitors with piercings and tattoos. They believe that the adults in their congregation pay attention to a look, and if you have that 'look' you are accepted (within the church), but if you do not, you are marginalized.

In this climate they feel like they do not want another lecture. "I don't always want to be taught. I just want to talk to someone." When the connection they desire is not met, it is easier for them to walk out the door. As far as many are concerned, they were wearing a mask and no one at the church was able to recognize it, so I will leave and seek out people who are interested in the real me. Another young adult referred to lack of connection to the older generation as they're "in cars, and we're walking. We see what they don't see" At this point, I guess we should have some older members providing cab service!

This need for connection in the church is not a small matter at all for the young adults who attend. Some of these young adults long for the days of youth groups and teen programs, reflecting "we don't do stuff like we used to" or they miss the activities in youth ministry. "I missed all the, like all the time that, all the fun time that we used to have back in the day" is the refrain of another young man from SB1.

Leadership challenges

Another issue causing young adults to not join in leadership is the shifting nature of leadership. Of the four churches represented in my focus groups, one was without a pastor, (although an interim is scheduled to start next month), one just lost a pastor (he resigned from ministry) and one has a pastor who will be districted (taking on the responsibilities of more than one church). Regardless of the real reasons why some pastors leave, the young people see it as leaving them, causing this response to a recent young adult female, "I think what makes people leave is that people keep leaving us. It's discouraging. You don't care." When the young adults feel like you (pastors/leadership) don't care about the church, they wonder why they should.

Along with shifting or changing leadership, there are concerns with pastoral leadership that is not led by the Holy Spirit. One of the focus group participants in SB3 made it clear that "(Pastoral) Leadership needs guidance by the Holy Spirit." There was a concern that their former leadership had a CEO mentality and they were not sure that the pastor should be the CEO of the church but should be looking to God as the CEO. "The church tries to preserve culture, but neglects Bible culture." Laments one young adult participant.

In another group, the young adults liked their leadership, but felt "they do what they want rather than what the church needs." Many of the young people liked their (pastoral) leadership but showed concerns for specific issues like "decisions made are personal, cultural, but not spiritual." And in one instance, a young adult was satisfied with the pastoral leadership at his church but expressed displeasure with members in power [who] may be going too far.

> "They take their leadership roles and start acting [more] holier than thou in that certain role that they have so it would go from just asking them to watch the door and have certain people coming in and out. And the next thing you know you're trying to get through the door and then they want your ID and birth certificate and everything else before you can even go into the church or out of the church or anything like that, so it's... other than that it's just how other people take their roles. It's like one

minute they're doing it for God and everything like that and the next minute it's um, it's just they want to command authority and stuff." – SB1

Some of the other young adults who were in leadership positions or are active in the activities of the church express feelings of being on their own because of sporadic leadership. So, they respond, "Let's see what we can do on our own." Or they are asked to fill in in some capacity in a program or worship service, one young man said, "Sometimes I felt like I could do it, others it seemed like I just happened to be there." There was no thought to him participating; he was just the guy who was on hand. This will happen in places where the leadership (pastors or department heads) were not good at planning ahead. For example, while I was with one of the focus groups, the youth leader of that church was planning the worship service for the next week and just filling in the names of the young people in the room with me.

And when this happens, depending on the relationship with the person asking, as one young lady resigned, "You have to do it."

Resistance to change

In an age of changing cell phones, Internet providers, TV shows, and latest pop stars, young adults are very used to the fluid nature of the world around them. They are challenged when they come to a church that does not embrace change easily. Granted, change in church is a process that cannot be taken lightly, but when young adults reach out and don't get support because of "old fashioned" attitudes, their attendance is affected.

Young adults also report that adults are not always receptive when we (the young adults) change, if they see you are good at something, they want you to do that thing all the time. "It's just praise dance you're so gifted. You should do this".

So, when I told people I want to go into science, they say "What?" Like, really." The young adults believe that the older generation wants things to stay the same instead of changing because, in their words, "They're naturally resistant to change."

Church not welcoming

Young people will not communicate with and seek help from parents, pastors, and teachers whose lifestyles and passions do not match their words and faith.[25] This quote is exemplified in the following response in a focus group

M– "It seems like whenever someone comes to church, they [the church] don't really welcome them [guest], they look at... they might say that, we love everyone and what not, but they still seem to have...(indistinct, too many voices)...if we bring someone in from the church. I saw a man sitting out there by himself. I came in and said happy Sabbath to him, he said" good morning". Then he went in church to look for a seat. He was looking around and I saw one of the older people that he looked at and make eye contact. He went like this (turning his head away)."

D– "You're kidding!"

M– "He went like this (repeating the previous action) The guy kept looking around for somewhere to sit and ended up sitting like in the seat right there (motions to his left) and no one around him was saying anything to him or anything."

These young people see their church as not very welcoming and as a result shun leadership. They believe that the adults at their church are acting hypocritical by not being more welcoming.

---

25 Kinnaman, David, and Gabe Lyons. 2007. *Unchristian: what a new generation really thinks about Christianity-- and why it matters.* Grand Rapids, Mich.: Baker Books.

Lack of young adults in attendance

This was frustration noted earlier from one of the focus groups & shared by the others when it comes to their feelings about the lack of young adults in their churches. One respondent believed that their peers needed to step and accept leadership, while at the same time admitting that he was not sure if God was calling him to leadership and that he would be involved, but only on his terms. This question of God's call can keep many young adults out of leadership because they cannot always identify what God's call is for them. This can prove challenging when as young adults, they have "the look" that meets the approval of an older generation but still feel that they are the same as those who may be looked at as outcasts or fringe because of their appearance.

Current leadership transfer

Among the churches reviewed, a nominating committee is normally the route that many local churches take to appoint new officers (leaders) annually or bi-annually. Whether your tradition uses a committee or if it is a decision by the pastor/priest, young adults seem to balk at being volunteered by the adults in the church. When asked about whether their church had a formal or informal way to get young adults into leadership positions, a young adult responded,

> "they're kinda slick with it. They'll first ask you to do small things like join the choir or oh just handing out these papers or uh go read a children's story or something like that. And then after they see you becoming comfortable then when the nominating committee meets they'll nominate you." – SB1

This wouldn't be a problem except more often than not, as a local university student noted, "For my church, they just sign you up for it."

Church members on nominating committees vote to add people to the leadership team of the church. Young adults are normally asked to either lead in youth group or to help in teaching children's bible classes. They are not normally looked at to aid in other areas of the church. The churches that claimed an informal and formal way of getting young adults into leadership are usually placing young adults in ministries that they expect that young person to be able to handle in the future. The challenge is that in these situations, the young adult is not always consulted before they are nominated, then they are pressured by well-meaning members to stay with it, all the while not being taught how to do what they have been nominated for.

Interviews

Over a period of 8 months I was able to interview 25 African American young adults ranging in age from 19 to 29. All of these young adults were in regular attendance at various black churches located on the west side of San Bernardino County. The majority of my interviews were in person, while four had to be conducted over the phone. Although the phone interviews could not be recorded, I was able to ask the interviewees to give me enough time to type their answers and I read the answers back to them to be sure we had an understanding as to what they meant. The 25 young adults interviewed represented views from 6 churches and broke down to 9 males and 16 females.

After determining a number of reasons why young adult were not in leadership from the focus groups, I conducted interviews with young adults to determine, well, how they feel about leadership? Was leadership at the church level something they cared about or even strived for? What I discovered was a good deal more nuanced than I previously thought. I also asked them if there was anything that the church could have done to assist them in their leadership journey.

Attitudes

When asked how they felt about leadership at their local church, 18% of the respondents answered with a positive answer, with another almost 22% willing to be involved in leadership. There was no central theme or story when it came to how they felt about leadership in their church. Not all of the respondents gave a clear answer as to how they felt toward leadership, at their church or in general. Some got lost in whether or not I wanted them to give me a review of their pastor or the people in their church. After some clarification, the clear answer was positive, with some nuances. There were the young ladies who were excited about leadership because they were the youngest leaders at their church and they also believed they had something to prove. The most curious attitude toward leadership in the local church was "shy away from the front". Those who claimed to shy away from the front were most likely to be willing to work in a team and wanted to be involved, they just did not want to be the person who had to make the report, if the report had to be made in front of an audience. They also did not want to have to be the one to cast vision, or direct anyone else to do anything. What they wanted was to work collaboratively on those things that they were passionate about. Those who expressed a feeling of pressure toward leadership also were unsure of self, although they were practicing leadership in one form or another. And although there were no outright negative views expressed toward leadership in the church, close to 10% not only stated "I don't want to be told I'm doing something wrong or looked at or judged" but felt unsure of self and not valued as adults.

According to the data, the attitudes of African American young adults toward leadership are positive. Young adults are willing to be in leadership as long as they do not have to be alone in leading. As with many young adults who work or may be students, their involvement in leadership will be limited because they don't want too much on their plate.

Practicing leadership

There were sixteen respondents who were involved in leadership presently, or recently at their church, school, or place of work. Those who said that they practiced leadership at their schools were mainly class project situations. A few practiced leadership through activities that were outgrowths of school activities (community service, internships, tutoring).

> "I have a class officer position at Loma Linda, in our class, and also in other student organizations." – DF

> "I'm in charge of the 'healthy neighborhoods' project, which is basically medical students and other students from the different schools in Loma Linda. We go out into the San Bernardino community and we have different projects." – AB

> Those who were involved in leadership at church were typically involved with leading children, youth, or singing on a praise team, "Where I work at school I lead a chemistry lab. Also lead on the praise team at church. It depends on what they need." - CD

> With some notable exceptions being of young adults who were voted to lead in an auxiliary ministry (other) at their church that was not a part of the youth ministry of the church. "In community service I'm the assistant leader, and we basically help the community with food and clothing. Last Sunday, we had an Easter program." - SS

More than half of those who were practicing leadership did so in the local church setting (56%). The fact that the number of young adults who got to practice leadership in church is significant because it lets me know that of all the places that have access to young adults, church is still a place where they can have an active role. So, when our young adults are not attending our churches, where are they getting their leadership development? I would posit that a lack of church involvement will create a generation of young adults who are not invested in anything.

Leadership definitions

In order to find out what the young adults believed leadership to be, I asked them two questions: to define leadership, and to tell me what leadership meant to them. From their answers there was a wide range of ideas as to what makes a leader. What stood out among the leadership definitions was an expectation that the leader be a good example, be responsible, and have influence. This type of leader we will call the "role model" leader.

The role model leader would be someone who young adults see as a good person. He or she may not know it all but is willing to let them in on what it takes to be successful, move forward, and experience fulfillment in their lives. This type of leader does not have to be charismatic, nor be the best at what they do. They must, however, be responsible in how they interact with people, and be trusted to keep their word. The role model leader is aspirational, someone the young adult would like to be.

The next group of definitions that came out in our answers were guide, takes initiative, visionary, passionate and character. This type of leader has no problem charting a new course. They are deeply passionate about what they believe in, or the ministry they are involved in. They can be counted on to have wild ideas, deep conviction, and contagious energy. I will call this type of leader the "pathfinder". The term pathfinder is particular for Adventist groups because we have a youth auxiliary that is tasked to do just that, chart a course and the curriculum that is used for the pathfinders is supposed to aid in the leadership development of teens, but does not always translate to the young adult realm of existence. Do young adults want to be pathfinders? Not if it means that they will be treated like teenagers again.

Our next leadership definitions include inspirational, prepare others, serving, director, good follower, and delegator. These leadership attributes we find more often in our pastoral leaders, or those committed to community service. I will call these the civic leader. The civic leader will be more interested in serving others. Their dedication to serving is inspirational; preparing others to do what they do is their lifeblood. This type of leader is effective among young adults who are interested in working in the church or in the non-profit sector because they get others involved in what they are doing. They do not rely on their personality, but it is the work of helping, the work of doing for others that fuels them to keep going.

Interestingly, the things that these young adults least associated with leadership were the things that I always thought embodied leaders: standing up front, mediator, flexible, and mentor. I'll call them the "traditional leader". Through investigating their attitudes, we may have found the types of leaders that young adults are willing to follow, or at the very least, who they will assist at the local church. This is not to say that a leader will not have these attributes or that these attributes are undesirable in the leaders that young adults will follow. What I am saying is that when asked to define leadership, these answers were not repeated, and weren't as strong in the minds of the interviewees.

What Should the Church Do?

The answer(s) to this question can provide the blueprint for what local churches can for their young adults in leadership. There were a number of responses to this question that made it seem that there were too many things on the list for the church to do. From "I don't want to be in leadership" to "support" there emerged a smaller and more cohesive subset that provided the information in a much more succinct and easy to understand manner.

What the young adults are looking for their churches to do is provide consistent and credible systems that will allow them to grow into leadership. Most churches don't have them. Of the young adults interviewed, only 1 made mention of mentorship at their church that allowed them to be familiar with having leadership at a young age.

We each had a leader as a mentor. We got to learn hands on with a mentor. I think to have a mentoring group would be an amazing thing for any church. Especially for those youth who don't seem to be interested in anything, to have somebody who was there already showing you is more reassuring. - SMB

These systems that can foster growth take into account the young adults as valuable members of the church, doing what they can to develop their talent so as not to lose them to another activity.

While systematic leadership transfer and training are something we can easily assume is needed, another outcome of this question was more positions for youth (18%). A better way to say this could be more opportunities to lead, and not just on youth or young adult emphasis days at church. One respondent recounted an experience of shadowing one of the leaders at her church:

> I remember from when I was younger, different churches that I had gone to that like, start grooming for leadership from very young. I remember once, when I was, I was like 8 years old, I was the junior treasurer that followed the treasurer around. So, I think it's something that you have to start kind of young so that they kind of get an idea of the different positions of the churches are, so they can also find out where their interest and talent lies. So, it's not just a last minute now we don't have anyone left so it's you now, go ahead. - AB

It's those opportunities afforded to young adults (and teens) to be involved before having to be forced to that go a long way to their involvement in leadership and having a vested interest in the success of the ministries at the church.

What should the African American local church do for its young adults? According to the data, the church should train, develop and support their young adults. They should be creating opportunities for young adults to lead, and then trusting them to do so.

Did your church drop the ball?

The respondents who answered this question were split. From a total of 15 responses to this question, 7 (47%) said yes, while 8 (53%) said no. Of the 7 who said yes, the reasons given for where the church dropped the ball had to deal with not having support, being taken for granted, and not being valued. One frustrated respondent stated, "if the church would have let us have more leadership roles we'd probably have more youth by now." While the feelings of another were expressed this way,

> "the mentality is what the older folk in the church say kinda goes. So, they don't really give the young people a chance to do stuff they would like to do. It's "this is the religion. [These are] the rules of the religion. Stick to it. Don't stray from it. This is how it goes." And you weren't able to go around stuff or cater more to the needs of your peers." - CS

Not all those who responded yes did so in anger. Most thought that their church was doing the best they could, and despite that there were areas where they could do better. Among those who answer 'No', they either had no expectation for the church to assist them in leadership development or felt that opportunities were present even if they did not take advantage of them personally. Since the majority of the responses were 'no' as opposed to 'yes' we can assume that church has not lost its role completely, but there is room for a more structured view of leadership development and ultimately, transfer.

Table 5.12 How did the church drop the ball in your development?

Taken together, the 'not valued' (29%) and 'no plan for me' (29%) bars on the chart speak to a need for young adults to be taken seriously by their parents, and older members of the church community. This desire to feel a part as a young adult is something that we will speak to in chapter 6. The church must be able to give room for the young adult(s) to thrive at the same time understanding that this period is very important as it relates to how they understand themselves and their roles in the church.

When young adults do not feel valued or that the Church has no plan for how they can meaningfully contribute to the life of the church, they are more likely to have a negative view of church leadership. They will not seek to be involved and may ultimately walk away from church all together.

What has helped in your leadership development?

Whether they were in active leadership or not, the young adults could attribute their development, if any, to a number of factors. Those factors did include church, work, school, and even home.

Table 5.13 where were you developed

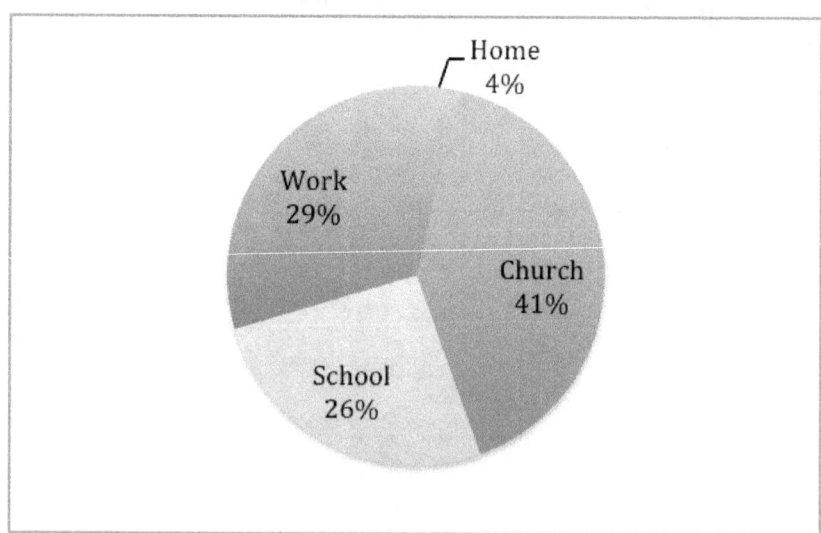

Although many young adults may not see the church as a large part of their development, the above pie chart shows from the respondents that the church had significant importance in their development as leaders. After seeing where they received development, there were some additional questions that asked how they were developed at school, work, or at church. What was done to assist you, or what did you learn?

> *For the one respondent who received development at home, they credited the relative with whom they live, "I think because of the examples I have in my life. My grandmother is very strong in her leadership in my home, but when she talks about leading she always reflects on what she has learned from her mother."*
> *– SMB*

For the other areas, such as church, work, and school, different things were gleaned from the interviews. For those who gave church as a place of development spoke to having a position, observation, and learning to be on their own as things they received as part of their development.

Table 5.14 Church helped develop

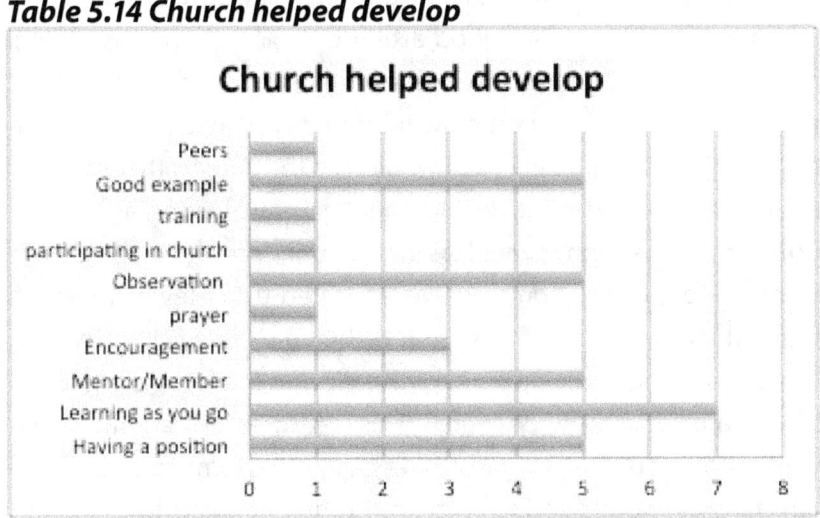

From school, the interviews credit specific classes and trainings. that helped them develop. Classes that had students work together in groups or had them present findings in front of their peers gave them confidence to believe they could be in leadership even if they were not in active leadership at the time of our interview.

Table 5.15 School helped develop

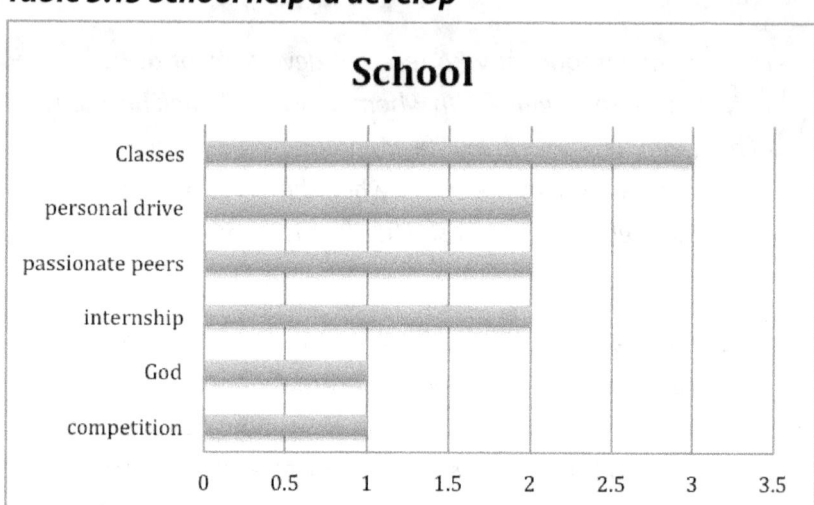

For those who cited work as a place where they developed, having a mentor (36%), having a good attitude (14%), compromise (14%), and dealing with authority (7%) were significant developmental tools gained in that environment. It is significant that leaders can be developed in many scenarios. I would like to contend that mentors still play a large role in the development of future leaders as we have noted in the mention of mentors in the workplace and in the church setting. More young adults, however, stated that they were left to figure things out on their own in the church setting (21%). This can leave the young adult with a negative view of the leaders while still having a positive view of church. This is further indication of what we found in our focus groups. Pressure to perform can adversely affect young adults and keep them from continuing to pursue or even be willing to be involved in leadership at the local level.

Table 5.16 Leadership development at work

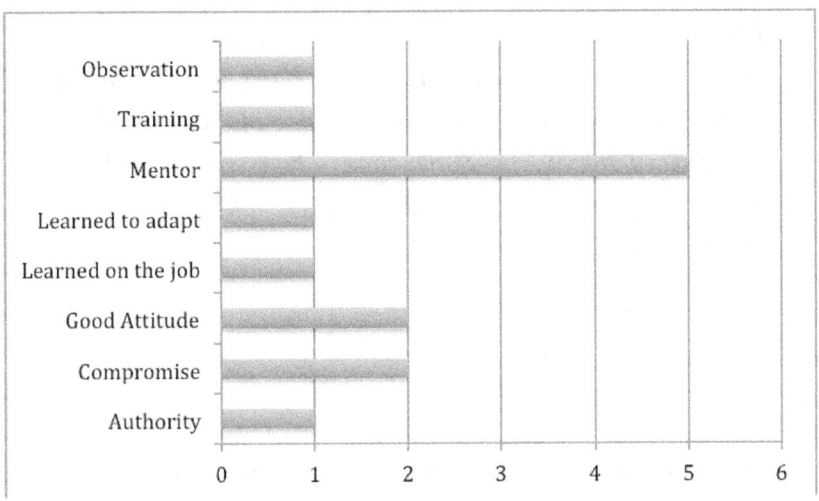

Leadership experiences

The respondents reported their negative and positive experiences dealing with leadership at church, school, and work. The majority (41%) reflected on their church experiences. Although I did ask about experiences at school and work, the church experiences were the most popular. This gives further evidence to how much influence the church can wield on the leadership development, or lack thereof, for African American young adults. As noted in the past, the church does still have a large influence on the church going young adult. When we (the Church) use that influence to empower and support young adults, we see more of them willing to lead on the local church level.

Negative leadership experiences were mainly characterized by conflict. That conflict could have come from the young adult acting as leader and not being able to motivate their people.

> *Sometimes the difficult thing for me as a leader was trying to compel everybody in that group who may not have had the same level of commitment or care, to move forward in a certain goal, or doing certain remedial tasks that you had to do over*

and over and over again in order to meet a goal or whatever; trying to get them motivated to do those type of things and do it proficiently. So, again I'm not the most vocal of people, so my personality kind of comes into it where I don't want to have to repeat myself, so that I think has been one of the most, that I can think of, the most negative times where what I would do in that situation, if they're not doing it, is to take it all on upon myself. – RW

A number of interviews felt that they were not valued as leaders, or even to be trusted to work without help or supervision from an older member of the church:

And she made this big ole, had this big ole meeting about how reasons why me and [young person] should not like, you know [be leaders]. And one of her reasons was "they're too young". And my mom was with me and said, "What do you mean they're too young?" And she was like, "Yeah they're too young they can't be by themselves." And she was like I don't remember if they were 18 or 19, and they were like "yeah they're 19" and she said "What?" I think she thought we were like 15 or 16, and I was like "we've been at this church for a really long time now" – AP

This speaks to another problem that seems to come up when we are looking for a transfer of leadership to the next generation. Unless this is the culture of your church, change will be slow in coming. Existing leaders find it hard to recognize young people as being able to contribute to the church as adults because they have yet to see them as adults and not just the young ones. In this situation, it makes sense to have a system to magnify the fact that youth have reached the age of adulthood.

Table 5.17 Negative leadership experiences

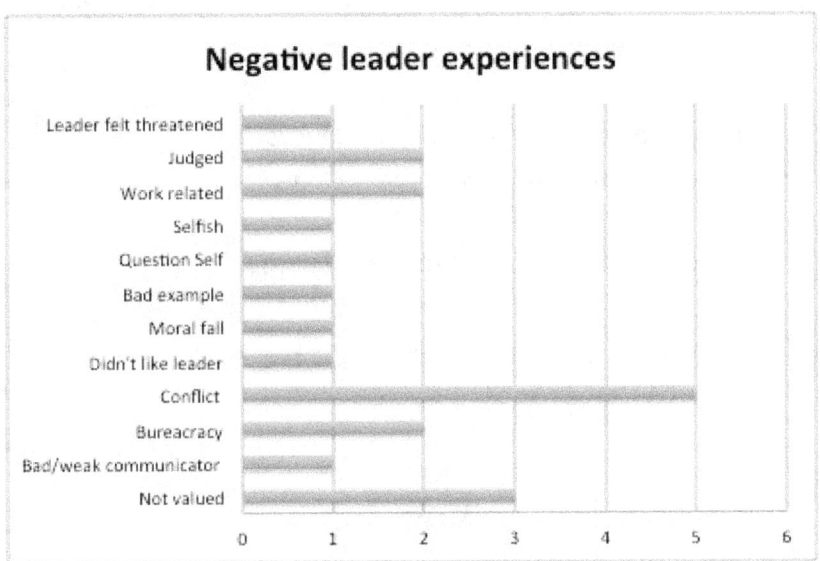

Our positive experiences recorded had the young adults enjoying successful projects with teams that were working together.

> "And just having that synergy between you as a leader and a person who is like-minded, you kind of have a backup. You have somebody who is working with you in the same mindset, towards a similar goal. So, uh, that situation it worked out really well, I wasn't always the one who had to step in and put my foot down, but I had someone who I could confer with and get their perspective" – DF

The young adults thought working with leaders who were friendly and approachable also made their experiences with leadership positive ones. When allowed to lead, and receiving support from the team or the church, young adults also felt better about leadership and leading.

Ever since I started going to [church] I got involved quickly getting to know people and the fellowship. I loved being voted as special events coordinator for the youth. I loved being the special events coordinator; planning events and having people who were older than me follow my directions. It felt good for me to see people happy with what I planned. – SMB

Table 5.18 Positive leadership experiences

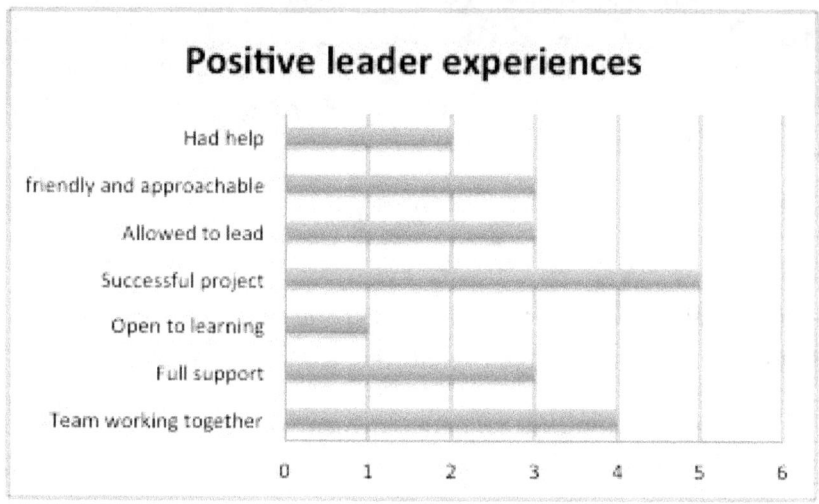

Summary

There are a number of reasons why the music of African American young adults is not playing in our local churches in San Bernardino County. These reasons include fear, pressure, lack of peer group and mentoring, church not welcoming, and resistance to change. Young adults want to be included in leadership more often than not. When they do not feel valued by the Church, young adults will gravitate to those places and people that give them support.

And with this knowledge the church still remains the place where more of our church going young adults can be impacted positively to be involved in leadership. The current leadership transfer of the Nominating Committee may need to be revamped in favor of a more organic change, where young adults can be included, trained, and/or mentored into leadership. Young adults are looking to be trained, developed and supported in positions of the church that may not have traditionally had someone in their twenties leading out. While the reasons for their lack of involvement are many, it is of particular importance for the local church to create systems that will help to make young adults take ownership of the whole church and not just youth ministry or music ministry. The attitudes of African American young adults are generally positive. They are willing to take leadership roles when there are systems in place to train, develop, and support them. There seems to be certain types of leadership that appeals most to urban young adults. These have been characterized as the role model, pathfinder, civic leader, or the traditional leader. Our task now is to seek out a system that can promote leadership development, possibly using an existing youth ministry model.

Chapter 5

FINDING THE MUSIC TOGETHER

Creating a new song

Culture often determines the kinds of music we listen to most. Many of us learn to appreciate the twang of country, or the lilting tones of folk music, but we all hold with in us that music that drives us when we want to truly feel alive. We use music to compel us when we need to exercise. Music is all around us. Jay Z said, "when you think about it . . . you realize that the beat is everywhere, you just have to tap into it."[26] We want to find the beat of young adult leadership and identify what the music can ultimately sound like.

In this chapter, the data from my findings informs a change in the development of new young adult leaders. I propose arguing the need for capacity building with the Human Resource frame and supported with the 5 practices of exemplary leadership. The challenge that I see now after reviewing my data is that there is no one program or practice that will meet the needs of all young adults. There are a number of programs that we can employ. We will then place my data against the existing successful models and see what would be the best fit in light of the needs of urban African American young adults.

---

26 Jay, Z. 2010. *Decoded*. 1st ed. New York: Spiegel & Grau.

A realistic future state of the African American churches in San Bernardino is to see a continuum of youth and young adult development. Ideally, the youth and young adults would feel valued and empowered at each level of church leadership. From the local church to the county (which does not exist), and to the Conference level, young people would have representation and influence. Young adults would be active as mentors to their high school and junior high brothers and sisters. At the very least, a competent youth leader (volunteer) or pastor (professional) at each church. These youth leaders would work together to develop a federation of youth and young adult leaders that would support the initiatives of the Associate Youth Director of the SECC.

Adults can gain immeasurable insight from youth if they would make themselves available to discern it. Input that organizations receive from youth partners can improve communities in a way that non-empowering communities cannot. In our situation, I would like to see our African American churches in the SECC improved because of the active involvement of young people and young adults in conjunction with existing intergenerational leadership.

In my future state, youth ministry would be committed to raising leaders from within the ministry. These leaders would then practice "reproductive leadership," meaning the ability to raise up and reproduce leaders from within the community.[27] These leaders would have the support of a community that sees youth empowerment like a three-legged seat; each leg of the seat would represent a vital aspect of true empowerment:

Opportunity – see youth. Youth all over the world have the potential to become empowered individuals, but only those who have opportunities will reach their full potential.

Skill – teach youth. We help those young people by teaching them necessary skills and highlighting their unique gifts, placing them in positions to be successful.

---

27 Arzola, Fernando. 2008. *Toward a prophetic youth ministry: theory and praxis in urban context*: IVP Academic.

Trust – believe in youth. Youth with opportunities and skills still need adults to trust them enough to gradually let go so they can do what they're destined to do.[28]

The responses from my interviews support the ideals of true empowerment. The young adults I interviewed want to see their churches provide opportunities for them to lead, but not necessarily in the traditional sense, meaning they don't want to have to stand in the front of the church to read or explain what they will be doing. They do want people to teach them and lead them in improving themselves in not only things that are applicable to church, but also applicable in life. They want to be able to trust their leaders and be trusted by their leaders to be creative, think differently about ministry, and how old traditions can be transformed by changing the tune.

This journey began for me as a question. In the subsequent years as I have been talking and interviewing, others have presented models that are successful in young adult ministry. I will review each of the top ten models and see which best fits in light of my research. We introduced the "top 10" earlier in Chapter 2, and with the structure of the human resource frame and the melody of the leadership practices I believe we can see a few musical arrangements that may work within an African American context.

The Top Ten and music development[29]

The Lost and Found Model[30]

Since this model predicated on the idea that every person is lost, it places a large emphasis on the gifts of the church or community of faith in reclamation. The Biblical basis of this model is found in Luke 15: the lost sheep, the lost coin, and the lost son. Each story has

---

28 Kelly Curtis, M.S. 2008. *Empowering youth: How to Encourage Young Leaders to do Great Things*. Minneapolis, MN: Search Institute Press.
29 The following models are found in one volume.
30 Evangelism, Center for Youth. 2011. Recalibrate: Models of Successful Youth & Young Adult Ministry. edited by S. Case: Advent Source.

within it a different circumstance by which one could be lost. One could be unaware, or aware but not able to get out of their situation, or so lost that you can be a danger to yourself. There is a celebratory aspect when a lost person is brought back to the faith. Young adults are always willing to engage in celebration, or party. Celebration is key to our exemplary leadership principles, where we are reminded to encourage the heart.

Although our African American young adults identify with many of their unchurched friends, they have made a decision to be at the church regularly and thus would not be looked at as lost. This model allows for young adults to be involved in ministry but does not provide opportunities for these same young adults to be prepared to lead in any other aspect of church life. So, while this would be a good ministry model for evangelism, based on what we heard from African American young adults, this would not make the grade for leadership development in the local church.

The Wholistic Worship model

This model looks at all of life as worship. We are in worship not only in our corporate gatherings, but also when we observe life, when we go to work, or when we sleep. This model seeks to incorporate worship into everything that the young adults are involved with. Our research didn't show young adults desiring a better worship experience, and that was not a part of study. This model, claims to be successful, but would be most impactful for African American young adults who may be seeking a better relationship with God. Perhaps worship retreats or learning spiritual practices in order to live in constant communion with God and be about His business.

The Discipleship model

Instead of a movement or event, discipleship is a journey. It involves coming alongside others, teaching, listening, verbalizing, questioning, testifying, growing and learning. The discipleship model values young adults by seeking to have them placed with a mentor and seeks their development thorough spending time and creating experiences. The disciple would then be engaged in a lifelong task of maturing as an SDA Christian.

Aspects of the discipleship model can be applied in our settings based on the needs of young adults to be valued and seek opportunities for growth. This model can also be used to address leadership outcomes by discipling the young adult toward leadership. So, while leadership may not be a primary outcome, the influence of the mentor can lead the disciple to want to disciple others on a small or large scale.

Through mentorship the discipleship model can integrate our five practices of leadership: modeling the way and inspiring a vision through interaction with a mentor. Challenging the process would be an ongoing revisiting of past issues also with a mentor. Enabling the disciple to act and encouraging the heart could be a combination of mentor encouragement and small activities created within the church community to further support the young adult. A church that would be willing to employ this discipleship model would be moving in the right direction to creating new leaders.

The Family-Based model

This model engages the family in an effort to return to what God originated in the Garden of Eden. Because many of our young adults are already living on their own, and are responsible for themselves, this model doesn't seem like it would be advantageous to the development of leadership or using the 5 practices. Young adults create for themselves family units among their friends from work, school, or church. Anecdotally can be seen in the use of terms like "brother from another mother" and "sister from another mister."

The Missional model

This model is based on the gospel commission to 'go' (Matt. 28:19-

20)[31], and the promise from God to fulfill it. Young adults are encouraged to share the gospel now in this world and with their generation. This model employs the practices of inspiring the vision, by encouraging young adults to be engaged in activities that would allow them to be the "hands and feet" of Jesus. There is a heavy reliance on God and what can be accomplished through the activity of the Holy Spirit in the life of the young adults.

On a secondary level, visionaries and people of faith can inspire young [adults] to be open to God and to place them where God can minister through them. Young adults would find their value in giving of themselves to others. This model allows young adults to seek out their own opportunities for ministry, but does not point to church leadership, or even focus on church activity at all. This model can feasibly have young adults constantly engaged in ministry but never engaged in leading in church. The leadership that is developed in this situation is one that is born out of sharing gifts and talents with others.

This missional model ideally develops young adults to learn new environments, getting to know others in their context.

The Social Advocacy model

This model presents as a community service model but moves to the reasons why people need charity to why aren't the homeless able to get work, or has the government not lived up to its obligations. Young adults do gravitate to causes and find value in being able to put their beliefs to work in helping others. This model relies on passion, perception, and perseverance. Young people have a general sense of justice, but often lack the depth of understanding or the experience to move beyond simple acts of kindness.

This model is also reminiscent of what we noted historically in the growth of urban youth ministry in the late 50's and all the way

---

31 *Therefore go and make disciples of all nations, baptizing them in the name of the Father and of the Son and of the Holy Spirit, [20] and teaching them to obey everything I have commanded you. And surely I am with you always, to the very end of the age."*

through the 60's. It can inspire, but without a good leader, this can be an exercise in futility that would ultimately do more harm than good. African American young adults desiring to feel like they have value may feel as if they have let others down if they are unable to be successful in this model.

This model also does not promote leadership within the church setting but creates community leaders. These would be leaders that are necessary for community engagement but would not necessarily be equipped to work within the local church model, unless we change the local church model. That is a conversation, and perhaps a book, for another day.

The Small Groups model

Size really does matter; the bigger the group, the greater the performance; the smaller the group, the greater the fellowship. These aren't guarantees; simply tendencies. While the small groups model creates an avenue for what could be discipleship, mentorship, or fellowship, its purpose is to further personal spiritual growth. This method is valuable in creating spaces where young adults could gain the confidence necessary to lead. Within the small group setting young adults can be nurtured and encouraged to learn their value. Small groups depend on a strong leader the commitment of those involved within the group. Without a strong leader, young adults will find something else to do. The leader or facilitator would also need to be a person that young adults believe they can or will be able to trust. 19% of the negative leadership experiences in my interviews were because of leader failure. Leadership can be taught within the small group, but it doesn't provide the mechanism to lead young adults into local church leadership.

The Cross-Cultural model

This model presents a 'unity within diversity' ethos. It claims that by being clear about the differences that we have as people, we can open pathways to helping each other in following Jesus. It presents a set of four needs:

1. **Awareness of Differences** – this includes discovering the needs, likes background, values, expectations, lifestyles, and orientation of those who are different than me/us.

2. **Acceptance of Diversity** – this involves being open to inclusiveness and embracing others.

3. **Agreement on Direction** – this might be a lengthy process, but the outcome focuses on working together to mutually meet needs. These needs could be to benefit an individual or the group as a whole, or something beyond the group.

4. **Application of Design** – this comes down to the practical sharing of experiences. Creating history together.

Within the African American churches, the collective story of people is repeated at least once a year. Where this model can be useful in the development of young adult leaders, young adults must be able to be aware of their differences between the youth (those younger than them) and the adults (those older than them). Accepting the intergenerational diversity in the church, creates an environment where African American young adults should be able to agree on a direction, or inspire shared vision. The key to this model is personal security or confidence in one's identity. This can be challenging when young adulthood is a time of identity exploration, instability, self-focus, and feeling "in-between".[32] One thing young adults can be sure of is that they are not sure of themselves. They do not have a strong, collectively shared historical moment that helped to define them and continues to shape their identity.[33]

---

32 Arnett, Jeffrey Jensen. 2004. *Emerging adulthood: the winding road from the late teens through the twenties*. New York; Oxford: Oxford University Press.

33 Robbins, A. and A. Wilner. 2001. *Quarterlife Crisis: The Unique Challenges of Life in Your Twenties*. New York: J.P. Tarcher/Putnam.

Young adults need to have people around them who can help them feel supported, in order for them to feel secure. Unfortunately, 35% of the interview responses in my research study expressed that the church did not have a plan for them, while 29% felt like they are taken for granted. Application of the Cross-cultural model seems that it could address that issue but does not create a platform for leadership development.

The Relational model

This model of ministry can also be referred to as "friendship evangelism." This model focuses on making relationship creation the focal point of the ministry. The true nature of the model is the relationships created, and not to increase youth/young adult group attendance. Our young adults who reported positive leader experiences had relationships that provided support (14%) or was approachable & friendly (14%). Having relationships like these in the local church can create an environment for leadership creation but does not necessarily get us the next generation of leaders that we are looking for.

Because the relationship model depends on one-on-one relationship creation, there will naturally be some people who are better at it than others. Personality can play a big part of who is being sought after in relationship building. Young adults can easily be caught up in the culture of a personality. The Mosaic generation epitomizes a me-and-we contradiction. To generalize, they are extraordinarily relational and, at the same time, remarkably self-centered ... they want to do everything with friends.[34] You also need a strong enough relational presence to make this the culture of your ministry model.

---

34 Kinnaman, D. and A. Hawkins. 2011. *You Lost Me: Why Young Christians are Leaving Church – And Rethinking Faith*. Grand Rapids, MI: Baker Books.

The Leadership model

According to the Leadership model, instead of voting young adults onto meaningless church committees, or making them leaders of ministries that are inactive in hopes of bringing life to them, allow the young adults to grow ministries from the church and recruit others to join them. We have an example of this from a few of the young adults interviewed,

> "I'm in charge of the 'healthy neighborhoods' project, which is basically medical students and other students from the different schools in Loma Linda. We go out into the San Bernardino community and we have different projects." – AB

> "I am leading out. There's a Dr. that works at the veteran's hospital that has a program. He takes inner city youth, and brings them to the church, and he does basically Sabbath school programs with them. I kind of took some of those kids and started a teen's class, because a lot of the program was designed for smaller kids. So, I just kind of took the older kids and started a program for that." – JS

This young adult got their friends to join in with what they were doing with the kids every Sabbath. Now JS gets satisfaction from serving the children from the community and having her friends be a part of the ministry. Her part in the ministry was not to start it, but she saw where it could be a little better. She wasn't required to go to a committee to get it approved. She took initiative to do what she thought was a small thing. The ministry continues, and she can begin to seek out the next leader from within the group or from her friends that join her.

Existing leaders should perpetually recruit others to join them in leading, and lead others to do so as well. No official mentoring labels must be assigned in order for mentoring to take place. Make it a two-way street with young people following and leading interchangeably, as needed and as the Spirit moves.

In order to make the Leadership model work there are two ways that we can go about it. One is when a young person responds to a need, like JS, she saw there was a need to have someone work with teens during the community Sabbath School. The other way is for an older member or existing leader to invite a young person to be a part and they are equipped to lead for the future. In the case of MN, she was asked by an older member/leader in the church to participate, and now she has led at one level of church activity and is willing to do other things.

The situation in which leadership takes place depends on at least one person following the leader. This happens all the time in unofficial ways, whether it's something as passive as participating or not participating in a given ministry, attending church or not attending, moving towards God or retreating from Him. A person's influence makes that person a leader.

Mentoring urban young adults

This area of mentoring is one that I've struggled with since being a volunteer in youth ministry. I have always sought out mentors to guide what my activities would be and how I was to comport myself in leadership at the local church level. And inasmuch as that was something that I desired, I never got that older church member to come along side me and walk with me. Yet here I am. What was the difference? I sought the aspects that I saw in others that I wanted to emulate, so in effect, I've been mentored by many and continue to be mentored now. Mentoring is not always about a one-on-one relationship. It can, as in my case and the case of many others, be an amalgam of interactions with people that we get to know over time. In today's climate, young adults are even more desirous of connection with people who can lead them into living the lives they imagine. The advent of social media and increased connectivity allows for more people to be led by a tribe of mentors.[35]

35 Ferriss, Timothy. *Tribe of mentors: short life advice from the best in the world.*

In working with urban young adults, I've thought it very important to have some aspect of mentoring involved. For me, I've spent time attempting to mentor those who I saw could replace me.

While some seek mentors, many of our youth are at best alienated and at worst completely separated from adults who can provide them much needed help. They do not choose mentors on their own, either because they don't see the importance of such a relationship, or because they don't know of any adults who would take that much interest in them. Either way, young men and women would respond enthusiastically, over time, to positive adult mentors.

From my own experience, and from what we hear coming from focus groups, and the young adults interviewed, for the local church leader there are some specific strategies that can be employed to grow leaders in the local church.

Select

There is a moment in movies or tv shows, when a band or team has to be put together, the progenitor of the team will be shown in quick cuts going from person to person. They will be shown walking to people in various areas of town with varied skills and backgrounds. One of the best looks at this process is the scene in Ocean's 11 when Danny Ocean (George Clooney) is getting the crew together with the help of Brad Pitt's character, Rusty. Throughout their recruitment of the other members of the crew, they discuss what their needs are and then go after the people who would meet those needs. Many times, in our church life, we don't go after what we need, and settle for what we have. There is always a need for the next generation of leaders. It is important that these young people are invited to be part of leadership, and then supported while they are learning leadership.

From the interviews, approximately 42% of young adults felt as if they were either taken for granted, not valued as an adult, or the church had no plan for them. I believe when older members take interest in the lives of the young adults in their church, these same young adults will take an interest in church. There should be a continuum of potential leaders being recruited by existing leaders. Constantly being on the lookout for new talent keeps existing leaders from becoming entrenched and can address the issue of people believing that their positions in church belong to them. Taking time to select or recruit youth and young adults into perspective leadership roles, allows for us to include them not only into the mission of God, but establishes a way to teach the mission of the local church.

Jesus exhibited a very tangible example of this process in walking through a familiar neighborhood and selecting the people who would be a part of his team. He knew the guys he was selecting. He had to have observed them from time to time in their spheres of influence. He had seen them at work, and even at play. And they (the disciples) had to have an idea of this man who had been seen around the town preaching, "Repent, for the kingdom of heaven is at hand." (Matt. 4:17) They may have thought "that guy is interesting", or "He's taking a risk, just preaching like that", maybe even, "I wish I could speak with that kind of authority." I don't know what was in the mind of those pre-disciples, what I do know is there was a knowledge of this Man, this itinerant Preacher who had taken over the mantle of John the Baptizer. When they were selected, they responded to the call. The Bible doesn't show them backpedaling, hesitating, or procrastinating. As a matter of fact, it went like this:

As Jesus was walking beside the Sea of Galilee, he saw two brothers, Simon called Peter and his brother Andrew. They were casting a net into the lake, for they were fishermen. "Come, follow me," Jesus said, "and I will make you fishers of men." – Matt. 4:18-19, NIV

The itinerant speaker, the fearless man, neighborhood walkabout, loaded at these guys in the midst of other activities and told them they could be more. He saw them and knew that there was more that they could accomplish than just catching fish, doing taxes, or farming. As a matter of fact, from the gifts they had already manifested He saw ministry. He selected them for ministry.

Being selected for anything is a special honor to the one being selected. Most of us can remember what it felt like to know you were selected for a team, a job, an assignment. It does something to the psyche when we are selected, even when we are selected for things we do not like! I'm an above average height male, but as a youth I was very average. So, when it came down to picking teams for any sport we were playing at the park, I was not usually a top draft pick. I also wore glasses with lenses the size of small coke bottles which did not do much for my athletic profile. So, whenever I was picked for a team, I truly was happy to be selected!

Young people in our churches need to know that there is someone who sees them, not for who they are now, but for who they can be. They long to belong. We as the older members, leaders, parents and friends need to see them in the midst of their activities and let them know that they can be more. We need to learn about their talents and gifts and be willing to let them know where they can be valuable in ministry and in the community. Being selected is more than just you're on my team. It has the power to change the trajectory of a young person's life. Being selected can create a relationship that changes a young person's view of the church and the world, yet selection to the team is not the end of the relationship. It is just the beginning.

Accept

When Jesus reached the spot, He looked up and said to him, *"Zacchaeus, come down immediately. I must stay at your house today." So, he came down at once and welcomed him gladly. All the people saw this and began to mutter, "He has gone to be the guest of a 'sinner.' "*
Luke 19:5-7, NIV

In Luke 19 we are reminded of what it means to not only be

selected, but to be accepted. Jesus is walking through the land of Jericho and is buffeted on all sides by the crowd. There are people all around attempting to get close enough to the Teacher. The recent healing of a blind man may have contributed to the crowd size growing.

There were two kinds of tax collectors, the Gabbai and the Mokhes. The Gabbai were general tax collectors. There was not that much graft at their level because they collected property tax, income tax, and other taxes that were set by official assessments, keeping the graft down as a result. But then there were the Mokhes whose responsibility included taxing of imports and exports, goods for domestic trade, and basically anything that moved on the road. They set the tolls on roads and bridges. Their assessments were subjective and arbitrary, basically, they could make it up as they went along. As a result, corrupt practices were the order of the day among the Mokhes. Zacchaeus was most likely more Mokhes than Gabbai. Within the ranks of the Mokhes, were 'great' Mokhes, and 'little' Mokhes. Zacchaeus was probably a great Mokhes based on Luke 19:2, *"Now behold, there was a man named Zacchaeus who was a chief tax collector, and he was rich."*

Zacchaeus was doubly cursed. Not only was he a pariah among the Jews, but he was also small in stature. While many today, don't make the same assumptions about short men, he would have been the object of hate because of his job, and ridicule because of his stature. Maybe that's the reason he took more than he needed to when it was tax time. Young adults live in a space where they are always looking for a place, 'where everybody knows your name.' And even if everyone doesn't know your name, there is someone (we hope) that will accept us the way we are. We all want not just to be selected, or picked on the team, but accepted for whatever gifts, talents, or even challenges we bring to the table.

He was a man "in between". The African American young adults interviewed felt like they were "in between". Those older than them as adults did not accept them, and they were too old to still be in the youth group. They wanted to be accepted by their church in a meaningful way but didn't have any formal way of making that happen.

Jesus, by declaring to go to the house of the pariah Zacchaeus, He instantly gave him credibility. It's like He said to the crowd, "You want to hang with Me? You have to do it at his house." It's important for leaders to not just be willing to let the unsung, the unseen, and the unloved hang with us. We have to make the overtures and the effort. Being willing is not enough when we are talking about building the next generation of leaders. Moreover, how many of us go to hang with them? Acceptance of others is a large obstacle to cross when establishing relationship with young leaders in any congregation. Far too many, don't think they are good enough, or that they even matter. Just imagine if more leaders made the attempt, like Jesus, to say to those on the fringes of our church community, our youth groups, or even adult groups, 'Hey, I'm coming to your house today.'

The new expectation is that people will first be accepted into the community of faith and their experience and learn about the Christian faith. Then in the process of belonging, they will come to a point of belief and finally learn to behave. (McIntosh 2002)

Model and Mentor

The three years Jesus spent with disciples is a window into a proper mentoring relationship. It's Jesus who selects His disciples although He is constantly surrounded by crowds of people. It is Jesus that shares His time with these young men who were not picked by any other Rabbi. It is Jesus who meets them where they are and invites them to follow Him. And in following Him they get the opportunity to sit at the feet of the best teacher who ever lived! Can you imagine just being around a man who embodied everything it took to be a man in every aspect of the word? He was a man culturally in that He was properly raised in a Jewish tradition. He was a man functionally because He had a vocation. He was a man socially because people wanted to be around Him. His manhood was not defined by what He took, conquered, or defeated. His manhood was exemplified by what He shared, who He cared for, and how He walked on this earth. He also took the time to pour into this disparate group of young men, each with a different burden and expectation of Him. He lived His life as an example for these men who would 'do life' with Him.

Even in the case of Zacchaeus, Jesus goes to "be a guest in the house of a sinner." (Luke 19:7) By going to Zacchaeus' home, Jesus demonstrates what it means to be a friend of sinners. In spending time with Zacchaeus, Jesus gives him the opportunity to learn from Him just like the disciples. He gets to watch Him in fellowship situations just like the disciples. He watches how He speaks and moves at this impromptu party at his home.

Leaders must be willing to share themselves with the youth and young adults in their congregations. We cannot be so fearful that they will learn about our mistakes. That's the point! Too many of our young people are led to believe that the leaders in their church haven't made mistakes, or questioned things in church. We have the responsibility to show our young people what we expect, and more importantly, why. One author put it this way, "Too many will reflect their teen years with disappointment and anger because of the absence of meaningful relationships with parents and other adults. Churches that provide mentor relationships as part of their youth ministry not only assist parents but also fill gaps in the adult community relationships with its adolescents."[36]

We, as leaders, have a responsibility to spend time with the young adults in our churches and in our communities if we want to see them succeed in leadership. We must give them the chance to see us model leadership as well as mentor them as they take on leadership roles. Jesus did as much when he took the time to answer a question from the disciples as it related to prayer,

"This, then, is how you should pray: "'Our Father in heaven,

---

36 McIntosh, Gary L. 2002. *One Church, Four generations*: Baker books.

hallowed be Your name, Your kingdom come, Your will be done on earth as it is in heaven. Give us today our daily bread. Forgive us our debts, as we also have forgiven our debtors. (Matt. 6:9-12, NIV)

Equip

The most popular leadership experience for young adults (positive or negative) was found in the church. While many young people in the world would reflect on their first jobs, or their involvement in extracurricular activities at school, it is in the volunteer opportunities in church impacted my research participants the most. The challenge comes when young adults have the opportunity to lead, their success will rise or fall based on how well they are equipped to take the next steps in their leadership development. This is chiefly determined be whether or not they are taught how to deal with conflict, and how supported they feel while in a leadership position. Along with being mentored, equipping our next generation of leaders is very important to the lasting success of the young leader.

Have you ever walked past a piano display in a mall or airport and imagine yourself being able to sit on the bench and begin playing some tune that you have in your head? Maybe you look at the piano and remember taking piano lessons or lessons of some kind with fondness, reminiscing and reflecting about 'what if' you had continued to play. The fact that you can't walk over to the piano and begin playing is because you are not equipped to do it. And if you are among those who could definitely walk over and play, I need you to imagine a different instrument!

People who are equipped to play in this situation are the ones who paid attention to their lessons. They are the people who spent time practicing so that when the opportunity was presented they would be ready. The responsibility of leaders in developing the next generation of leaders is to never forget the lessons that need to be taught. We need to be mindful of the equipping that has to take place in preparing our youth and young adults for leadership. The equipping at your church does not need to be exhaustive, but it does need to be practical and essential. What do your young people need to know to be in leadership in your church? If you've done your job in equipping your youth and young adults, then the Bible gives us a promise that will seal the work that you have put in:

> But the Comforter, <u>which is</u> the Holy Ghost, whom the Father will send in my name, he shall teach you all things, and bring all things to your remembrance, whatsoever I have said unto you. (John 14:26, KJV)

At this point in their development, young adults are beginning to strike out on their own, seek long term companionship, and use the skills learned in school and translate them to the workplace. The local church must be willing to take up the responsibility of training young adults for church leadership. How can the lessons of Sabbath school and youth group now be applied to leading in a particular aspect of church ministry? Part of this equipping must be the teaching about all work done in the church is ministry.

In the church where I serve, we've recently changed the intentions of a popular evangelism meeting to have the speakers teach our young people skills. Every child, youth, and young adult had the opportunity learn a particular skill to be applied to their lives right now. They would not have to wait until they were older to apply the principles they learned on those days. In fact, they would be able to sharpen their tools with every day as they used the information given to them. Our churches have the opportunity to not only develop young leaders to impact our worship and church business but change the community around us because of what they learn in the 'house of prayer.' (Matt. 21:13, Mark 11:17, Luke 19:46)

Send for service

The last phase of this discipleship paradigm is service, specifically send to serve. When leaders have been selected, accepted, mentored, and equipped, it is time to do the work. It's time to get into the lives of others, either to repeat the process or serve them as a result of what you have learned. The church, therefore, should serve as a sending center. I think we can see as much when we return to the music produced in the life of Zacchaeus.

Upon spending time with Jesus of Nazareth, Zacchaeus exclaims, "Look, Lord, I give half of my goods to the poor; and if I have taken anything from anyone by false accusation, I restore fourfold."(Luke 19:8) He is willing to serve every person that he has ever mistreated, and not only that but to give them four times the amount that was taken from them! There is something powerful about the Presence of Jesus that compels us to want to work in His name. Leaders who have experienced the SAME (Select, Accept, Mentor, Equip) things that Jesus did for His disciples cannot help but have a desire to serve the body of Christ or even the greater community. These people become leaders who will not leave your church because of a disagreement over a vote. These leaders have been prepared in the fires of trial and error in the music room of your church and now they are ready to play their part in the grand orchestra.

The last message given to the disciples of Christ who experienced the SAMES model was to go and replicate what they were able to experience: Then Jesus came to them and said, "All authority in heaven and on earth has been given to me. Therefore, go and make disciples of all nations, baptizing them in the name of the Father and of the Son and of the Holy Spirit, and teaching them to obey everything I have commanded you. And surely, I am with you always, to the very end of the age" (Matt.28:18-20, NIV). I maintain that the purpose of the church and the believers in Christ Jesus the risen Lord should be to be 'sacred sending centers.'

The sacred sending center is the place where believers are able to be discipled in the SAMES way that Jesus did what He did. The leader of the sacred sending center realizes that the people who attend have been allowed to learn the music of Jesus: they have been chosen and recognize that they matter in the ministry of the church.

Chapter 6

OUTRO

Emerging adulthood

As a function of their emerging adulthood, young adults are in transition. The local church can be a powerful influence on young adults when they are valued, supported, challenged, and mentored. I learned that because many of the African American young adults were in transition they had needs that the church could meet as long as the church understands they need each other. Young adults have the need to be treated like fully realized adults despite their lack of experience, to know that the church will support them through this time of uncertainty and opportunity. It is important for young adults to know that they belong and that their friends are welcome. Affirmation from the local church and its leadership is very important to the esteem of young adults. Young adults need opportunities to see that their potential can be reached through service in the local church & community.

When the local church shares values with young adults they are more likely to stay. Church members need to create connection with the young adults in the church and not just the pastor or the youth pastor.

Successful models

I was introduced to 10 successful models of youth and young adult ministry from the Adventist literature. Of the 10, only 1, the Leadership Model, had the outcome of creating leaders. The foundation of the human resource frame and the 5 practices allows for the creation of a culture that would bear young adult leaders. These leaders would be empowered and trained to be mentors to the next generation creating a system of reproducible leaders.

Suppose I don't fit?

The descriptions of the types of pastor's young adults follow is not definitive. What I detail above is just what came from my research. Suppose you don't find yourself in one of the descriptions above, does that mean that you cannot lead young adults or that they will never follow you? I don't believe that to be the case. If you do not embody the same characteristics as detailed, you can still be a strong advocate for young adults and they will follow you. There are some strategies, if employed on a large or small scale, will gain credibility with the young adults in your congregation. Three things that will change their view of you: create community via the Internet, study the culture of young adults, and learn to lead with transparency.

Internet Community

Traditional leaders tend to be late to engaging with the Internet fearing the technology's dark side. This is especially true within Adventist ranks. There was a time when going to the movies was listed as a "sinful practice of the world" or "soul-destroying amusement". These ideas tend to keep traditional leaders from readily using the internet to foster community. For these leaders I would suggest two ways that they can engage their young adults: create a Facebook page and start blogging regularly.

With young adults increasingly choosing to forgo church

involvement, many churches are waking up to the need to embrace technology as one more effective tool.[37] Creating a Facebook page or a regular blog will increase your profile among the young adults in your church and allows them to engage with you in a way where you can still set the ground rules. Blogging allows for you to write about, let's say, your most recent preaching series and invite young adults to respond. Having a Facebook page allows you to see what your young adults may be involved in and what moves them to write and update their profile. The Internet will never replace real community that the church can provide, but it gives leaders a window into what young adults in their congregation are thinking about and possible subjects to tackle with the church as a whole.

The Internet also can make you aware of trends in pop culture that can have a negative effect on the lives of young adults. It would be necessary to perform cultural exegesis to teach young adults and the church at large about how trends are interpreted through the lens of Scripture.

Cultural Exegesis

Seminary study and undergraduate theological degrees prepare pastors to exegete the text of the biblical record in the original languages, learn about historical implications and customs that inform the characters of pre and post Christ eras. The same acumen developed to study Scripture can be applied to studying the culture. That is called cultural exegesis. It is the practice of looking for the deeper in the mundane. Culture, according to Miriam-Webster, is **the customary beliefs, social forms, and material traits of a racial, religious, or social group.** Being able to identify what cultural norms young people are exposed to helps in how we model what it means to be a leader.

---

37 Stetzer, Ed, Richie Stanley, and Jason Hayes. 2009. Lost and Found : the younger unchurched and the churches that reach them. Nashville, Tenn.: B&H Pub. Group.

You can identify and contrast what leadership looks like in the context of school, work, family, and church. Culture not only embraces the church but is especially targeting emerging adults dealing with transition and starting to get a hang of how the world works.

When I was in Seminary studying youth ministry, exegeting culture was a regular assignment. As long as you are working in an urban environment there are going to be aspects of that environment that we have to parse through using a gospel-centric lens. As you are developing who you are selecting and how you will accept them, consider taking a thoughtful hour every day delving into the culture of your youth and young adults. In this way, you are familiarizing yourself with the things that young people are exposed to through media and their social groups. There are books that help in the discipline of exegeting culture:

- *A Matrix of Meanings: Finding God in Pop Culture* by Craig Detweiler and Barry Taylor
- *Reviewing Leadership: A Christian Evaluation of Current Approaches* by Robert Banks and Bernice M. Ledbetter
- *Reel Spirituality: Theology and Film in Dialogue, 2nd ed.,* by Robert K. Johnston
- *Hip-Hop Redemption: Finding God in the Rhythm and the Rhyme* by Ralph Basui Watkins
- *Personal Jesus: How Popular Music Shapes Our Souls* by Clive Marsh and Vaughan S. Roberts

This list is by no means exhaustive, but can put the leader in a position to better engage emerging adults, those termed as nomads and exiles and show them where Jesus has already appeared in their everyday lives.[38] By showing Jesus in the everyday, you can now

---

38 Kinnaman, David, and Gabe Lyons. 2007. *Unchristian: what a new generation really thinks about Christianity-- and why it matters*. Grand Rapids, Mich.: Baker Books.

show the emerging adults of your congregation that you can be authentic and real.

Transparency

Another way of looking at transparent leadership is to lead with authenticity. Young adults in your congregation want to know that you will not be fake with them or the church. In a media landscape that is filled with reality shows and scandal magazines, young adults want to know that the leaders they see and want to become are real. The following is a good rule of thumb when it comes to leading transparently to affect emerging adults toward leadership.

Leadership is about motivating people to achieve meaningful and purposeful things in their own lives and also in the lives of others. Being transparent literally means to "allow the light to shine through." Put them together – leadership transparency is influencing others to change and make an impact by allowing the light to pass through who you are.[39]

Being transparent does not mean that you are making your life an open book, but that you are willing to open the book of your life for further review when the need arises. It is about being willing to share your hurts, hang ups, heartaches. It involves being open and honest with a purpose – a purpose that is redemptive and developmental, a purpose that allows the light to shine through who you really are so that [young adults] are impacted[40] to be leaders in the local church.

Even if you do not find yourself having all the traits of the types of leaders that urban young adults would follow, all is not lost. As long as you are willing to use social media to create connection, use your study skills to exegete contemporary urban culture, and are willing to be transparent you can still have a positive effect on the young adults in your congregation and prepare them for leadership.

---

39 Stetzer, Ed, Richie Stanley, and Jason Hayes. 2009. Lost and Found: the younger unchurched and the churches that reach them. Nashville, Tenn.: B&H Pub. Group.
40 Ibid.

Author Bio

Delroy A. Brooks, DMiss

Delroy A. Brooks is the pastor of the Juniper Ave SDA church located in Fontana, Ca, where Love abides. Formerly the youth & young adult pastor at the Valley fellowship SDA Church, Rialto, CA for 8 years. He is a graduate of Oakwood College (now University), the SDA Seminary at Andrews University, and a doctorate in Missiology from Fuller Theological Seminary. Pastor Brooks is happily married to his wife of his youth, Dilys Brooks, Campus Chaplain at Loma Linda University. Their union has produced two blessed children Micah and Matea who want to move to Australia someday. He is avid cultural critic and sports fan.

Connect with Author

  @dayufpasta

 https://dayufpasta.wordpress.com/

www.ingramcontent.com/pod-product-compliance
Lightning Source LLC
Chambersburg PA
CBHW052103110526
44591CB00013B/2328